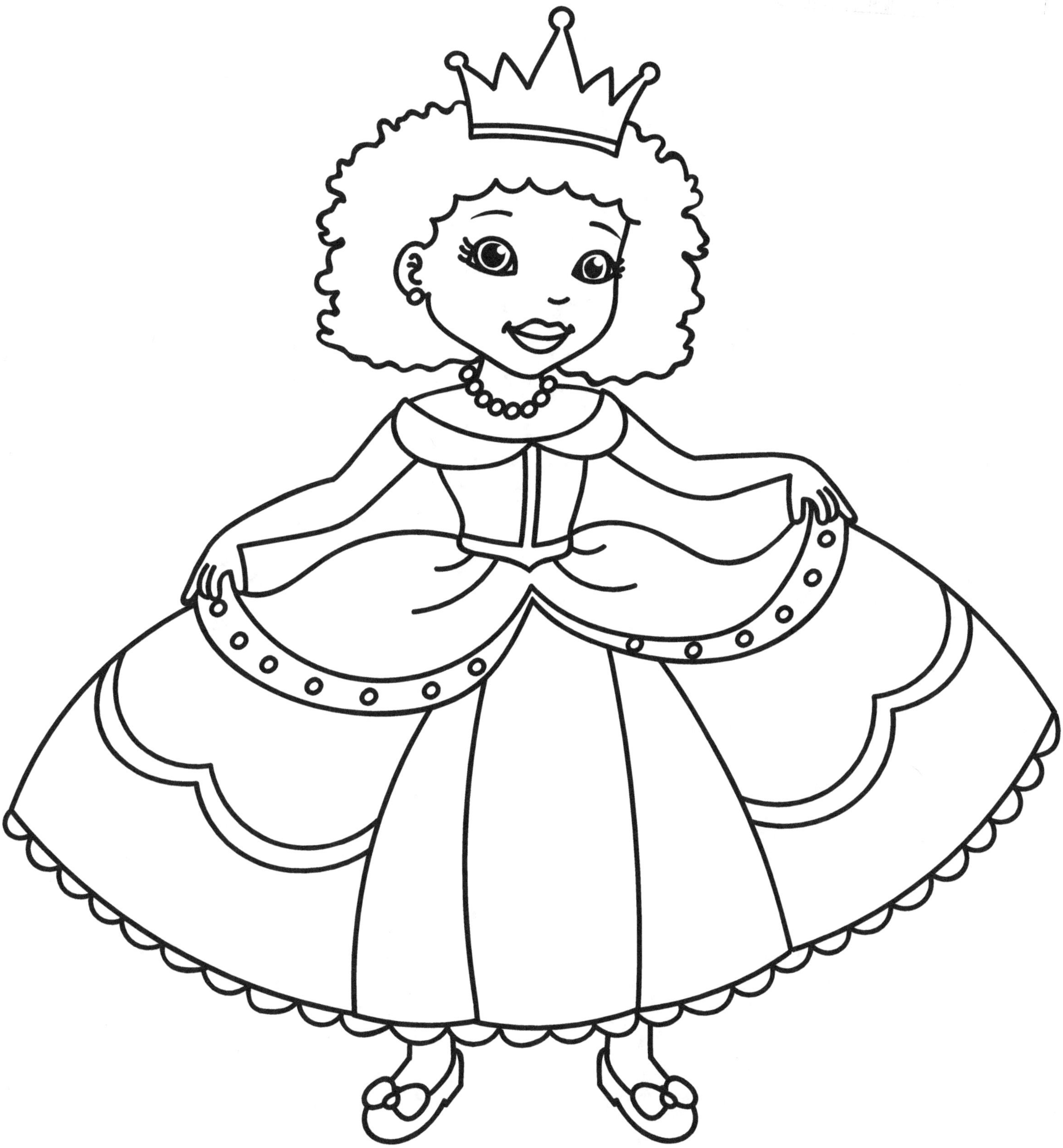

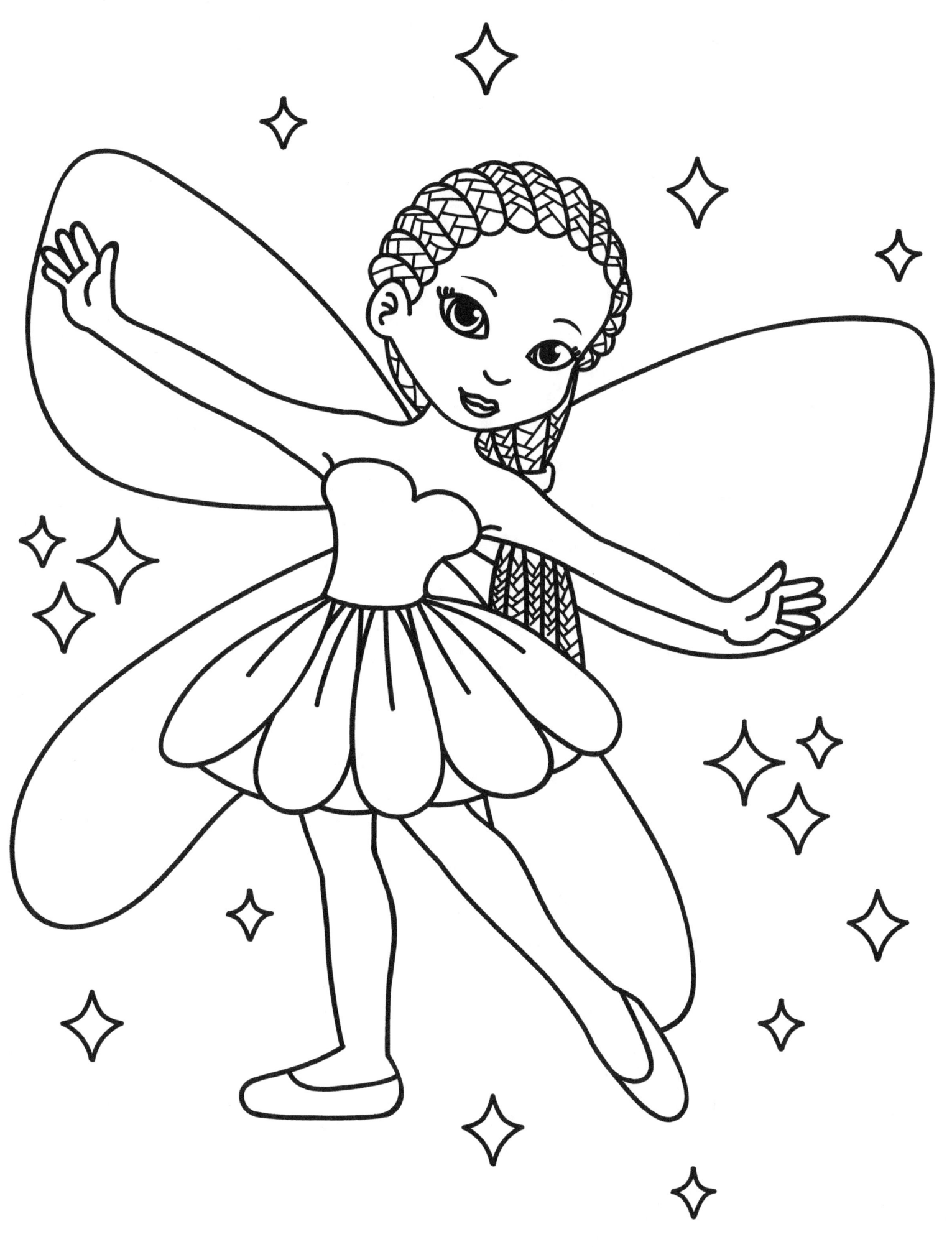

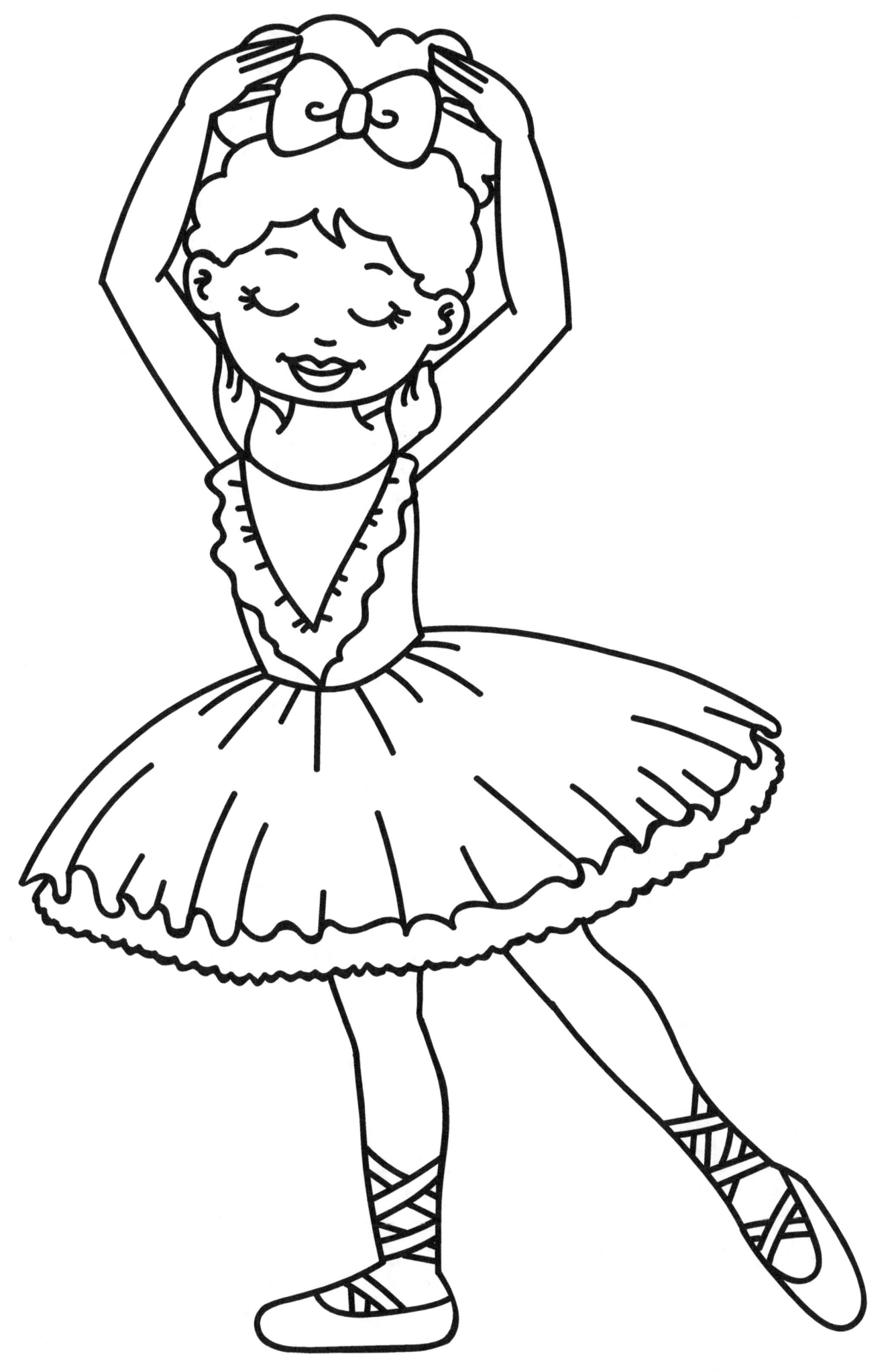

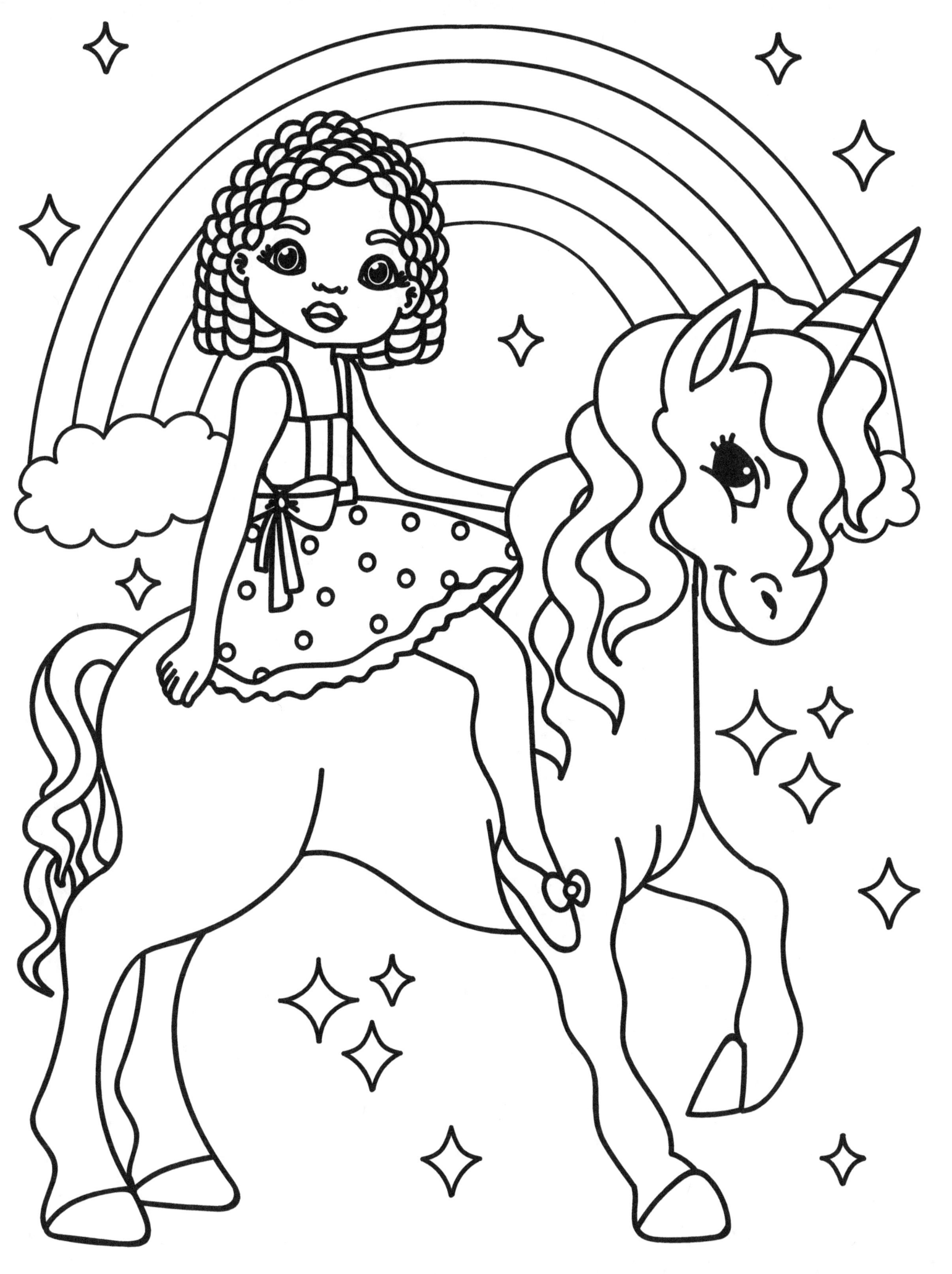

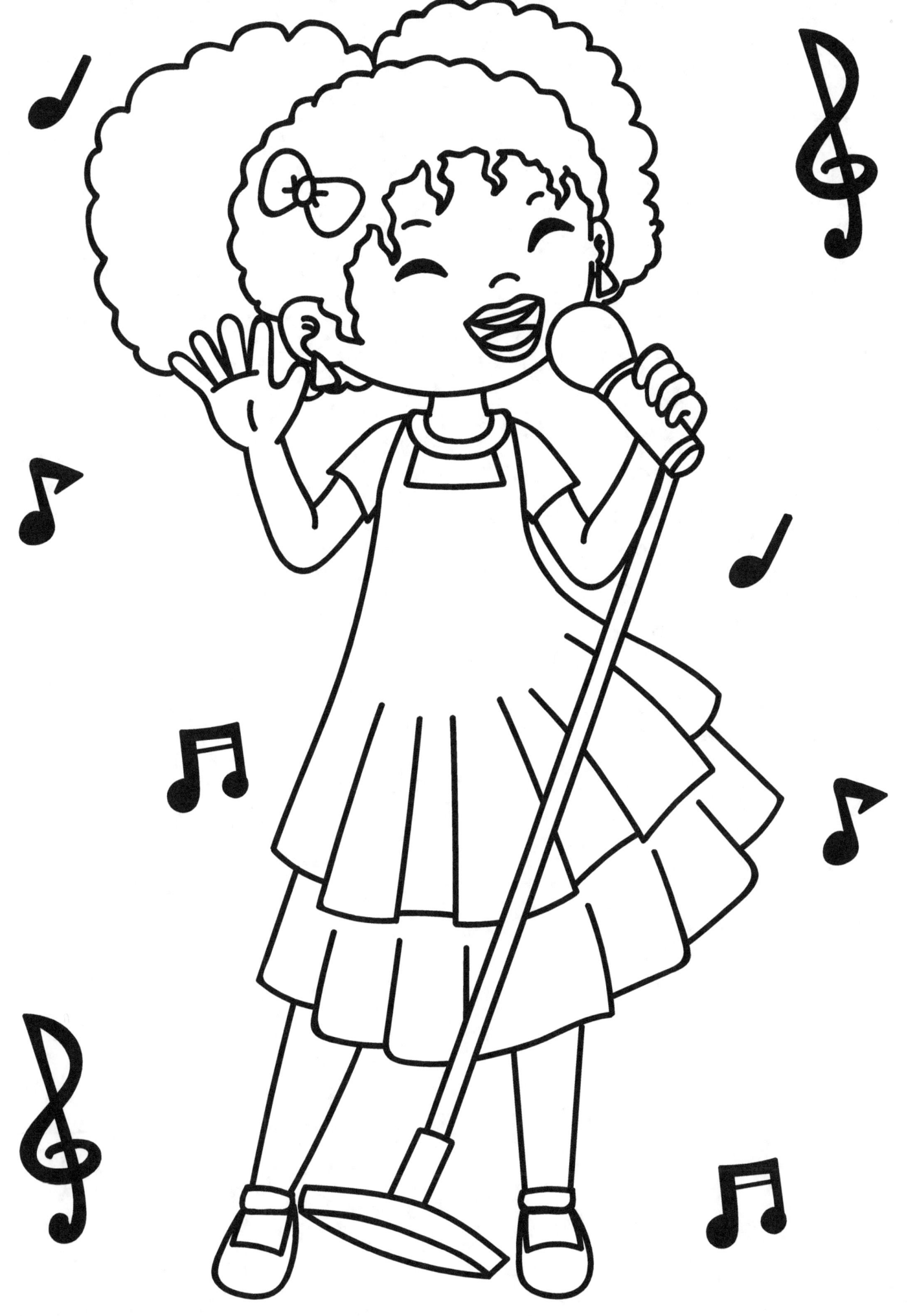

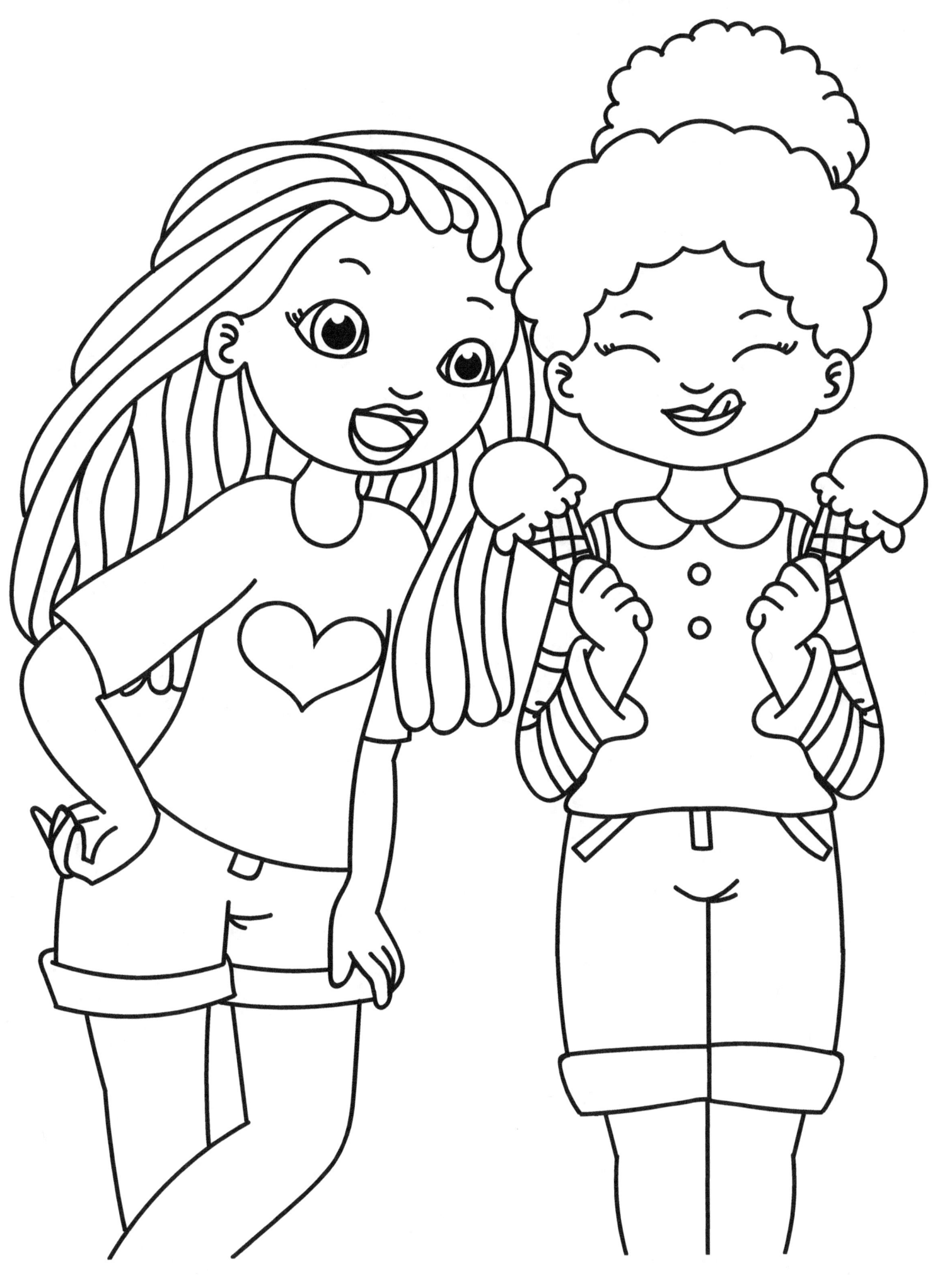

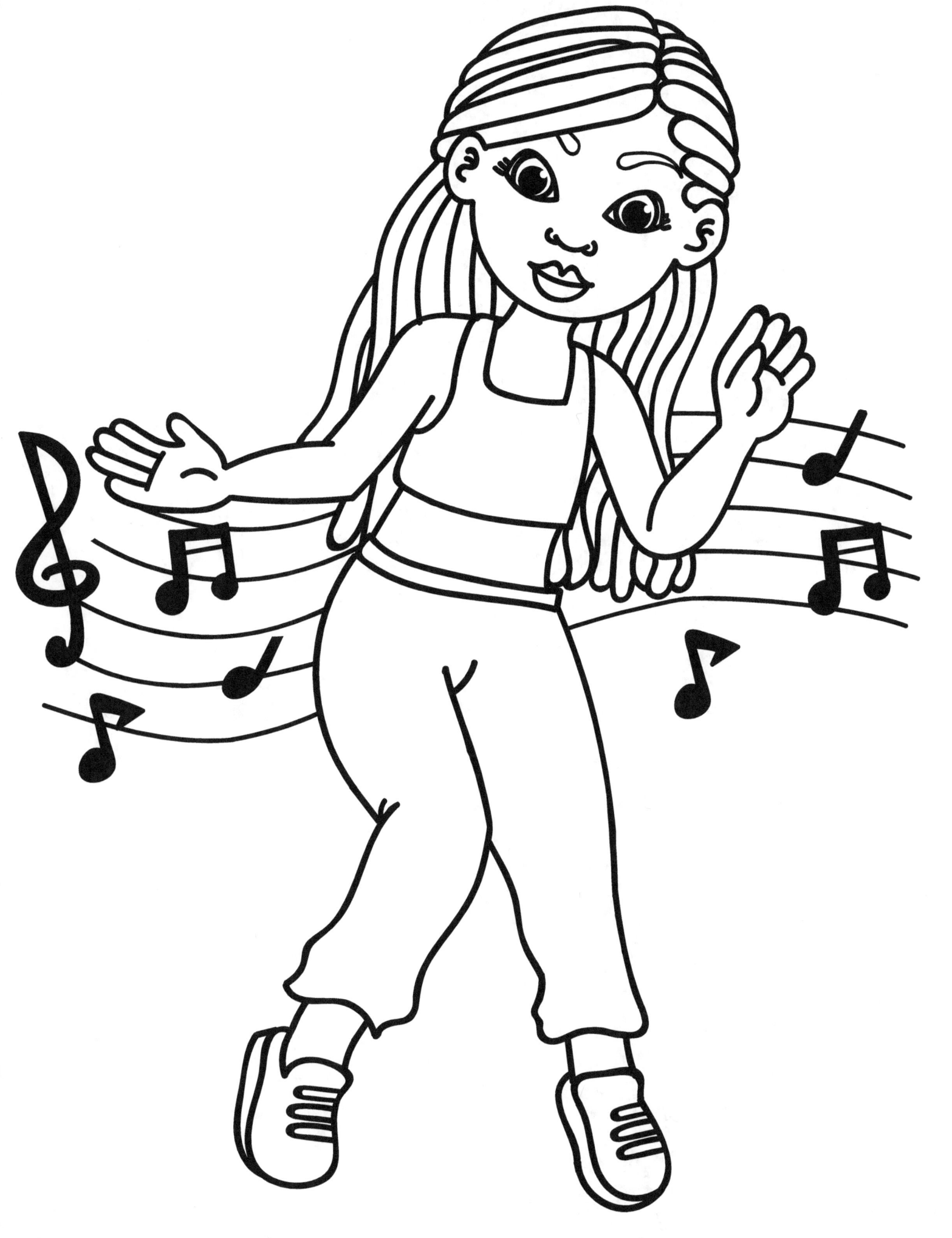

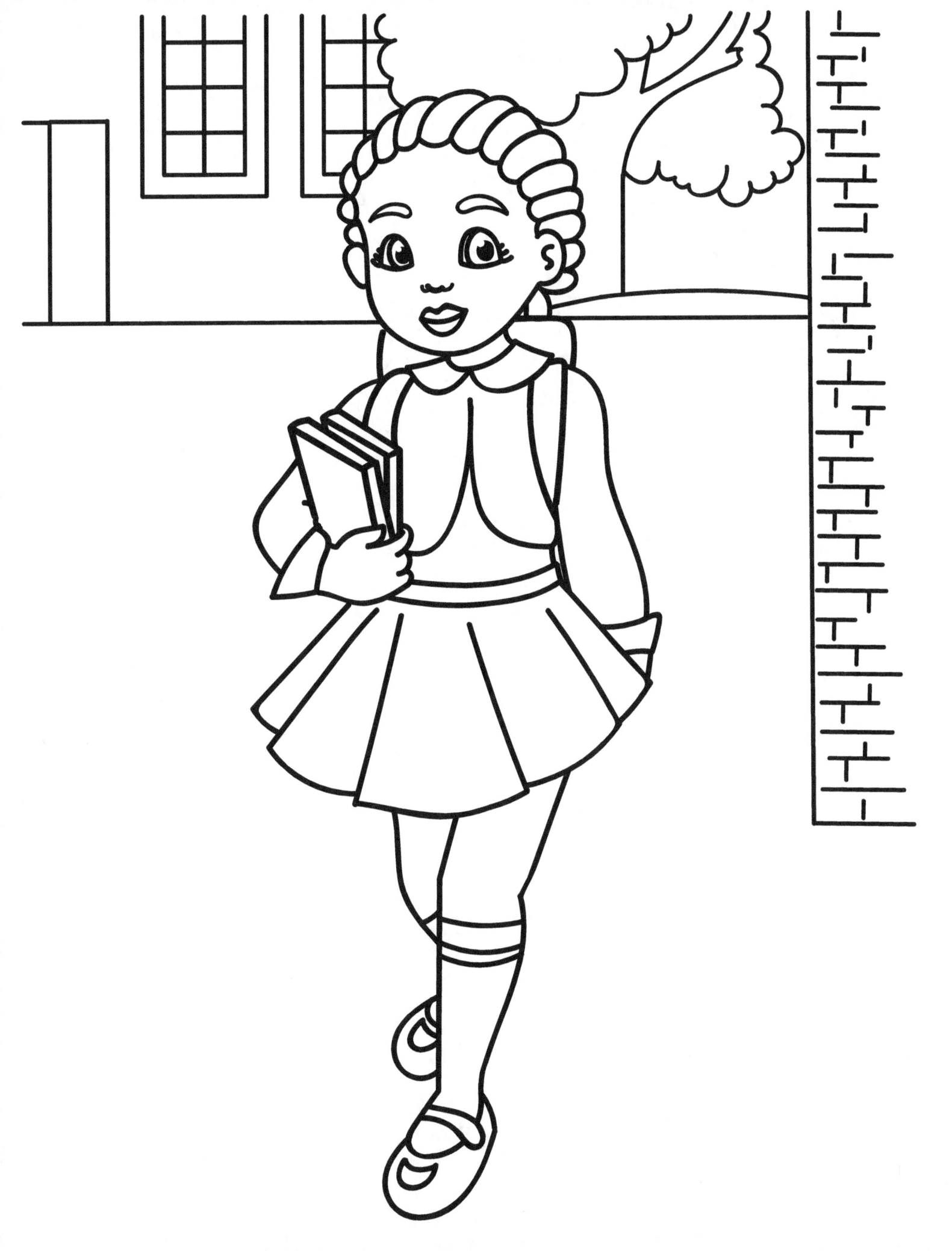

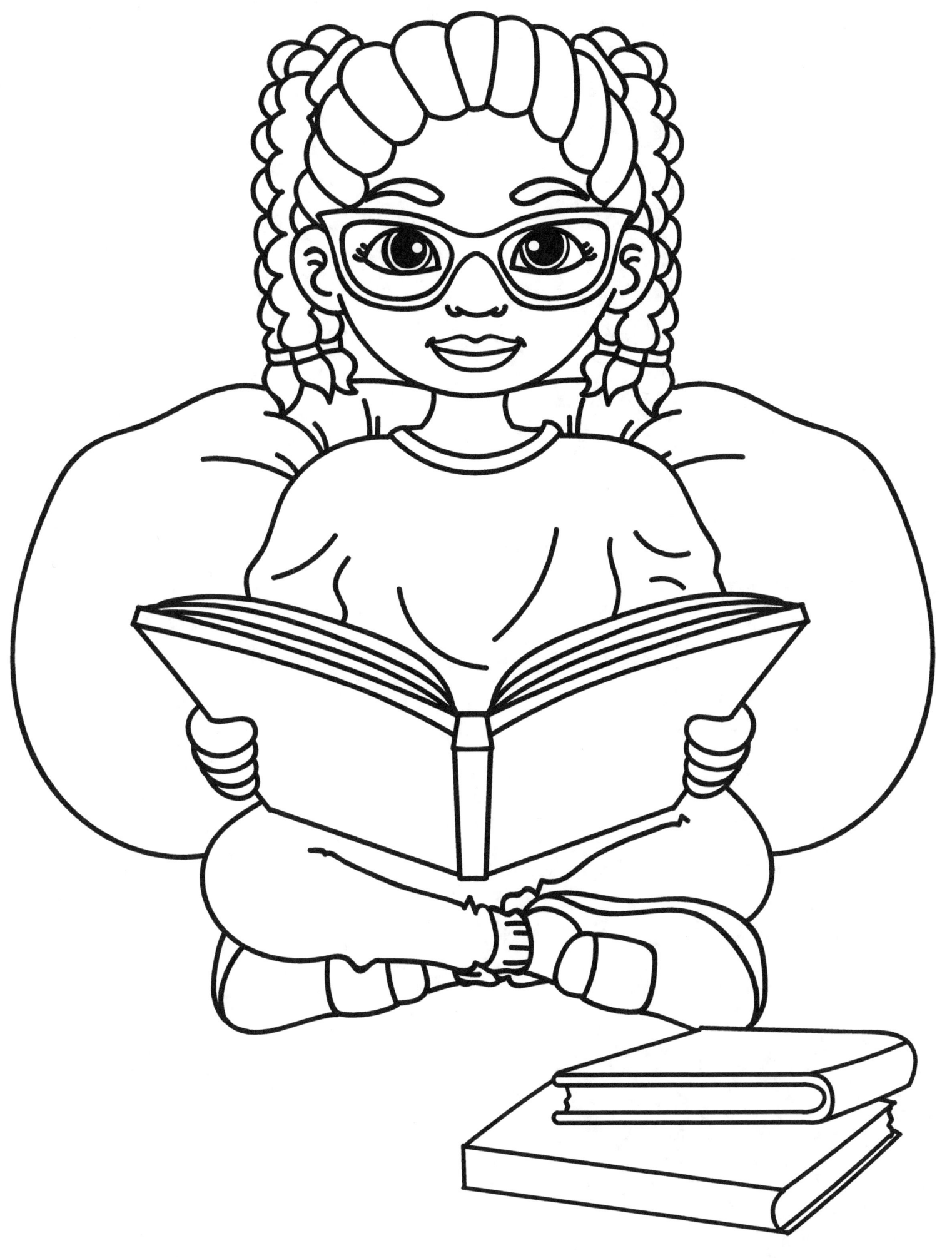

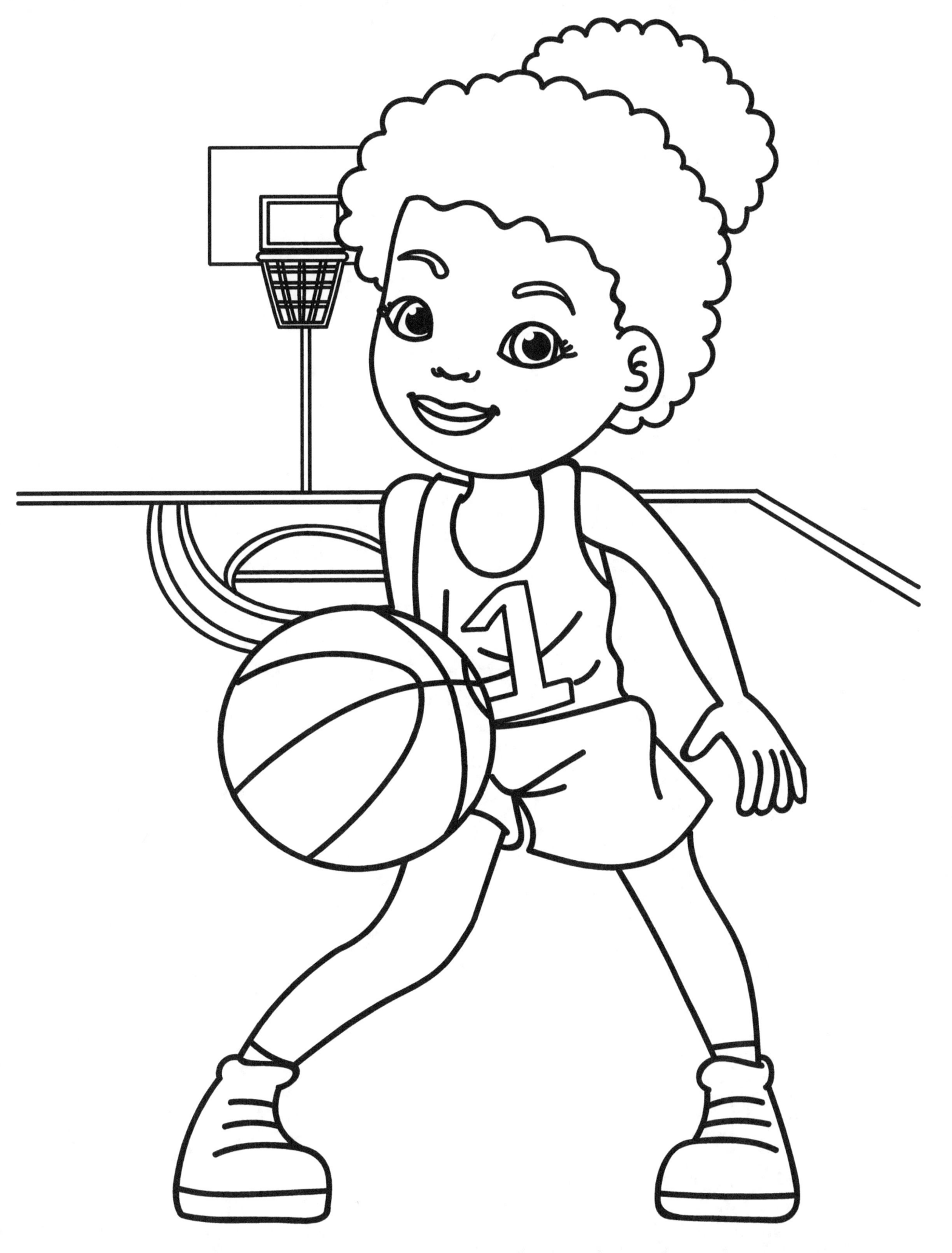

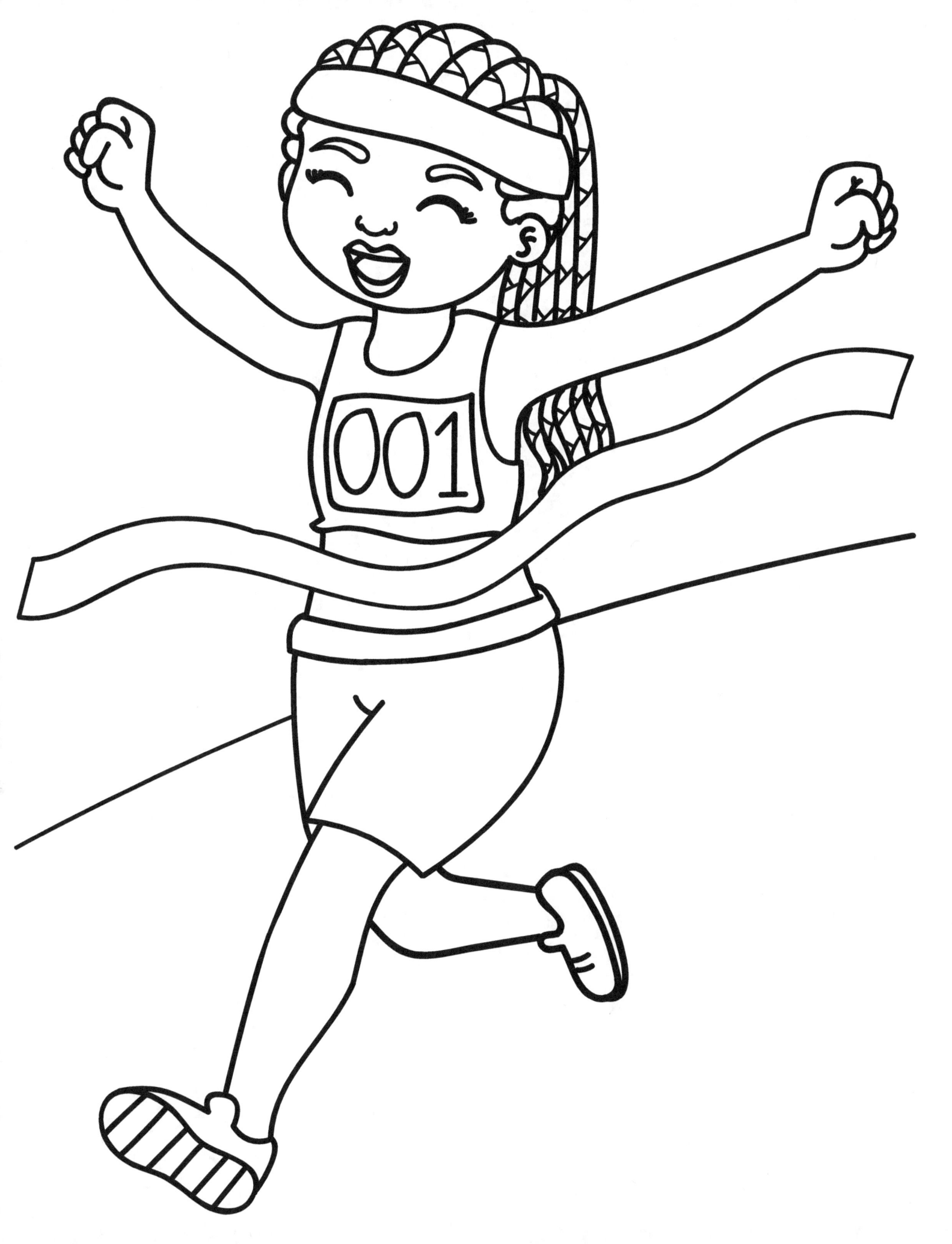

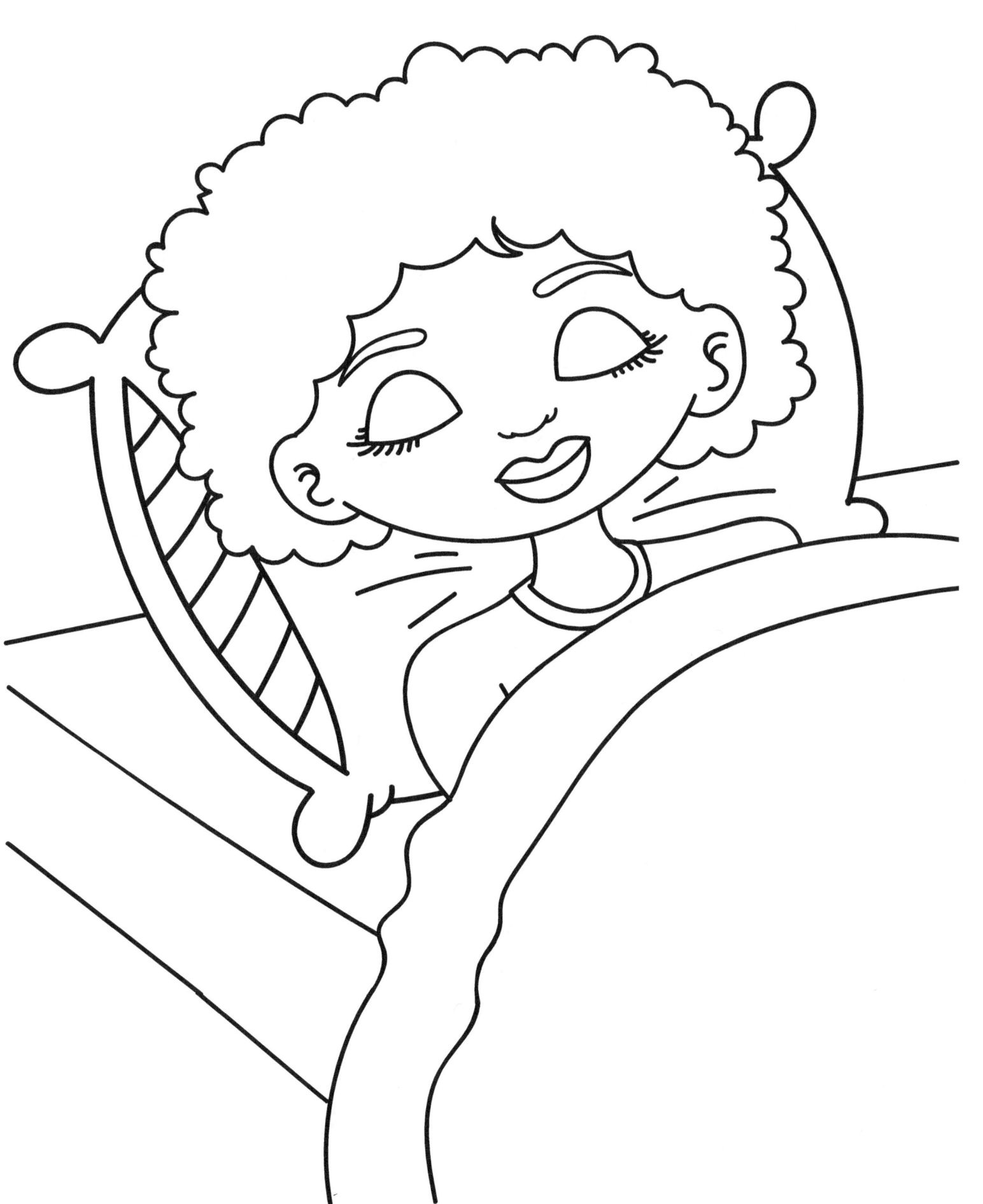

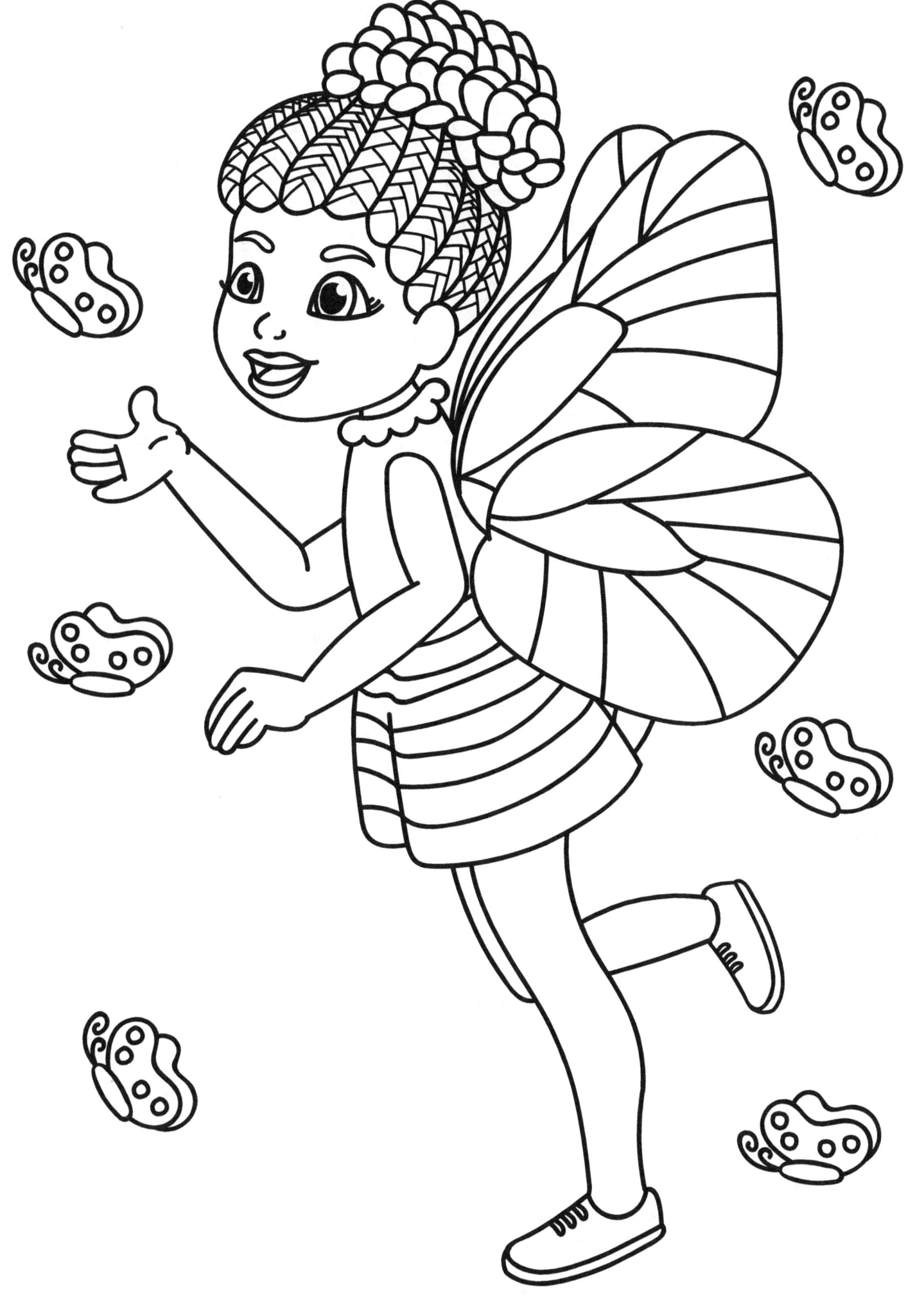

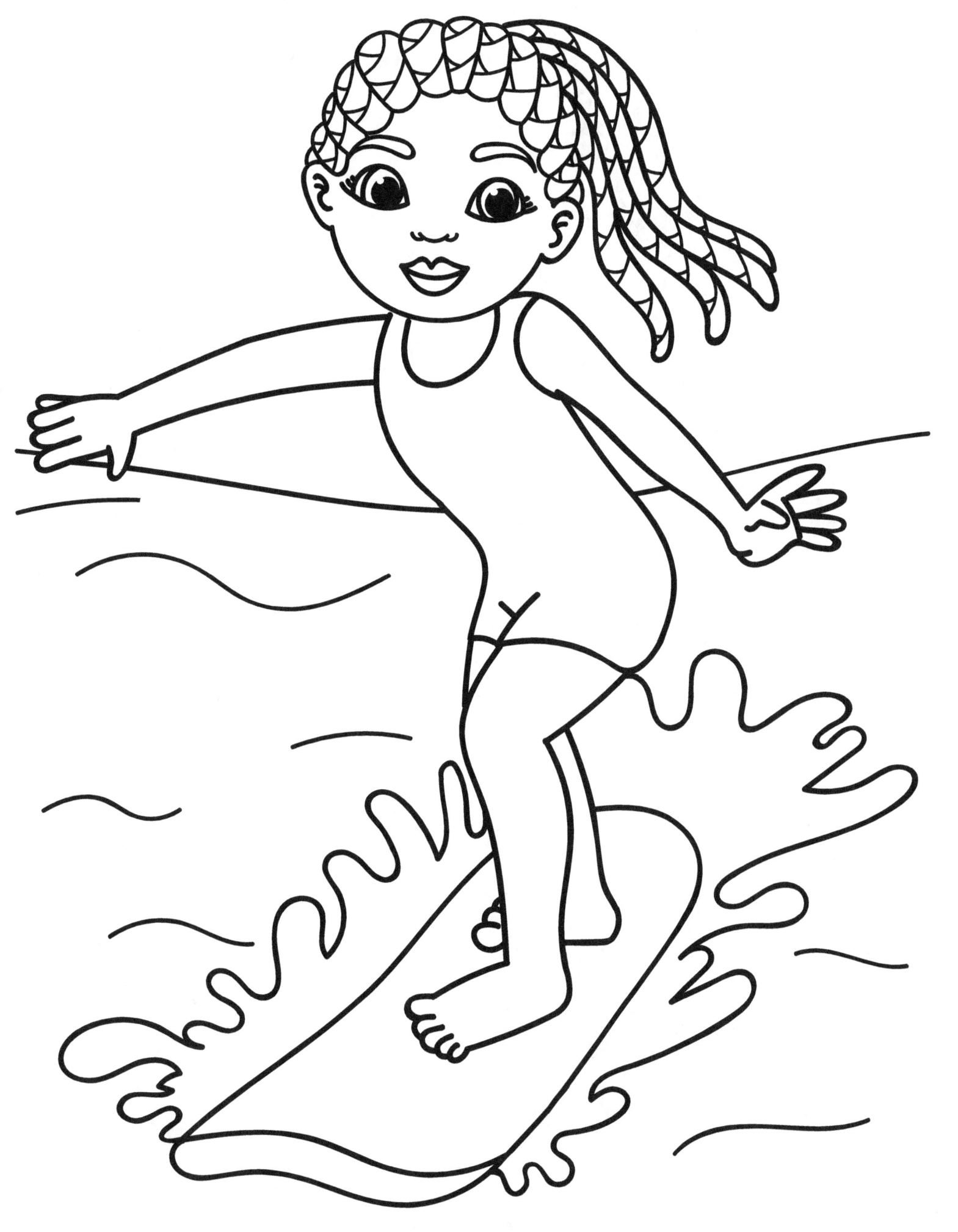

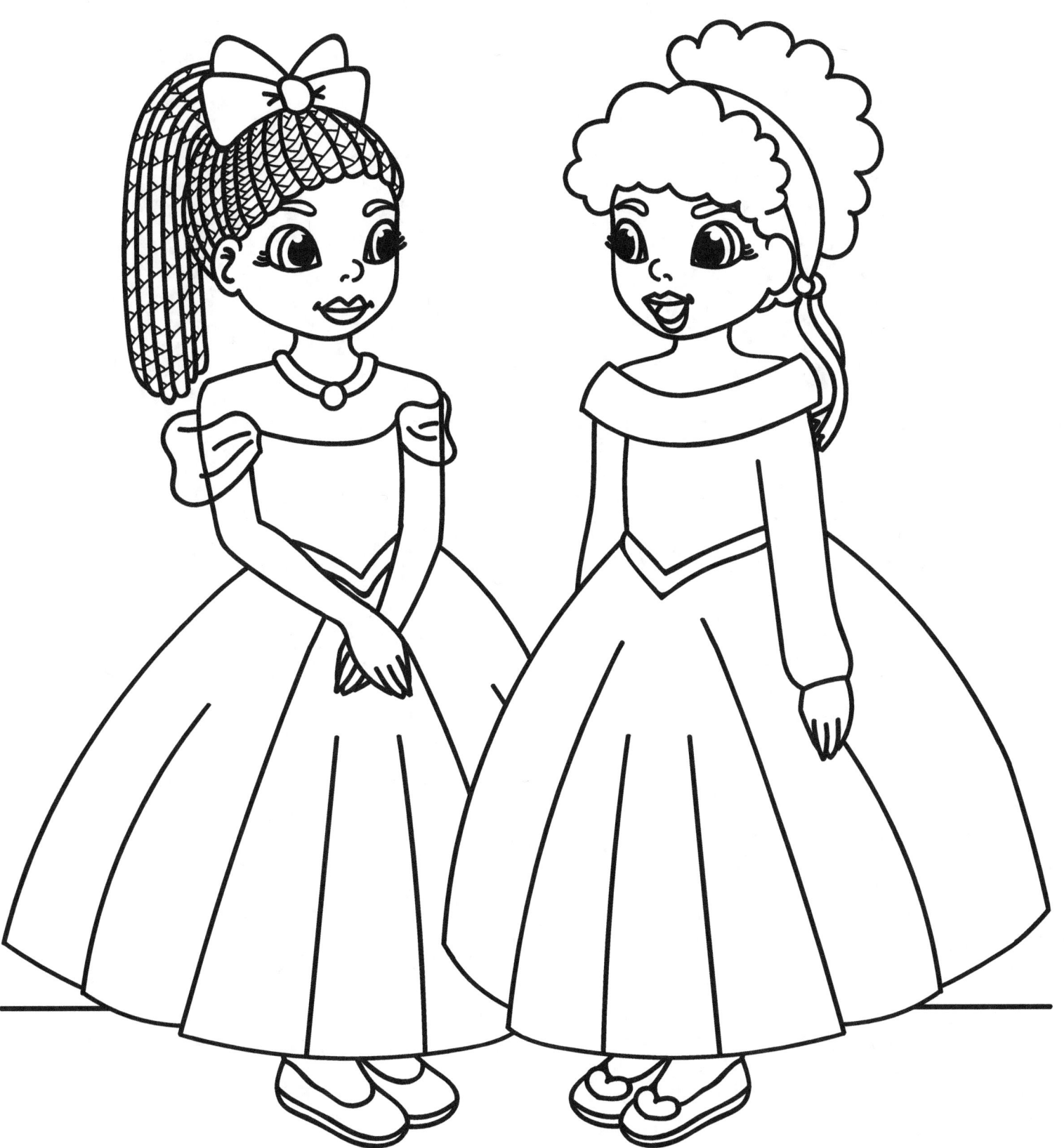

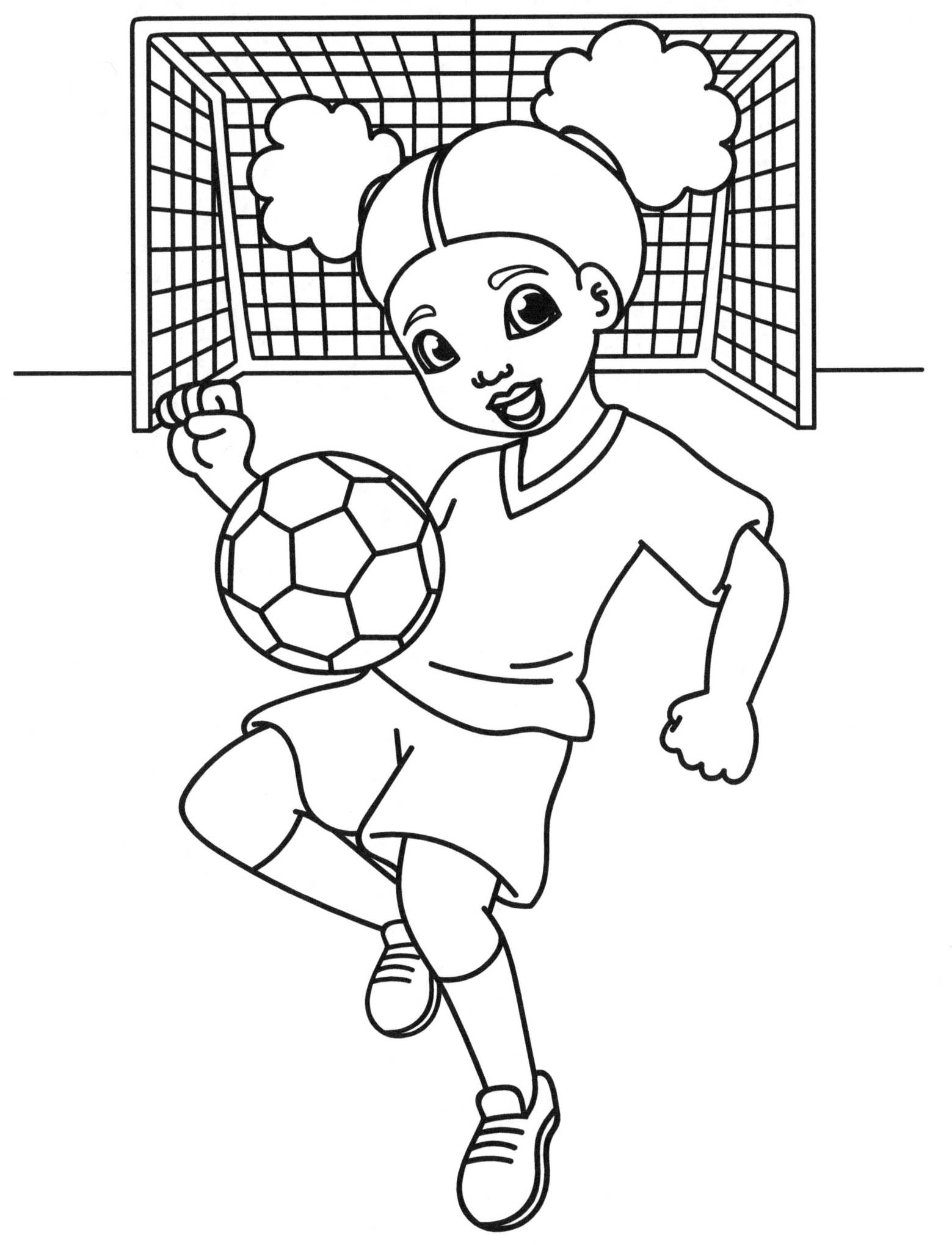

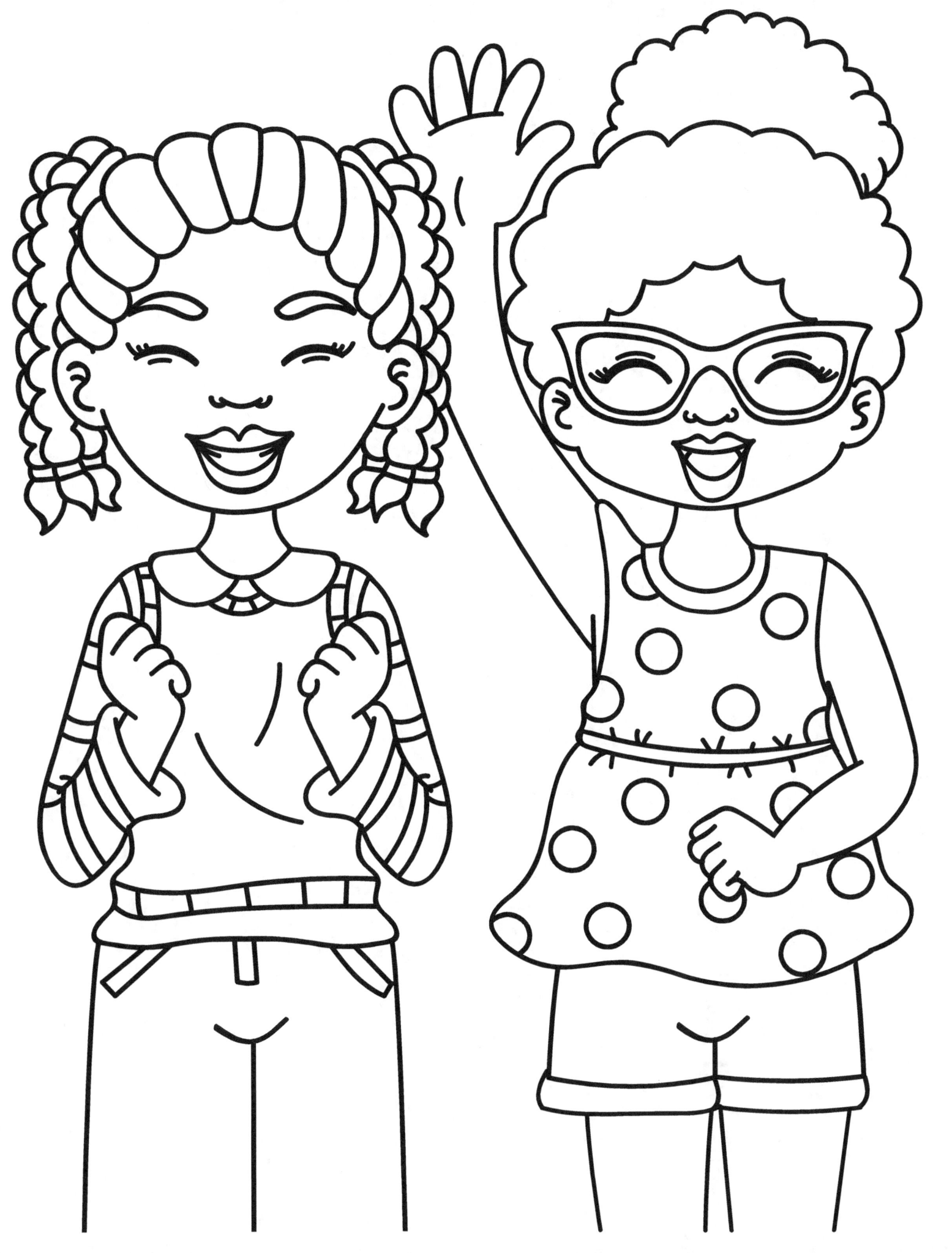

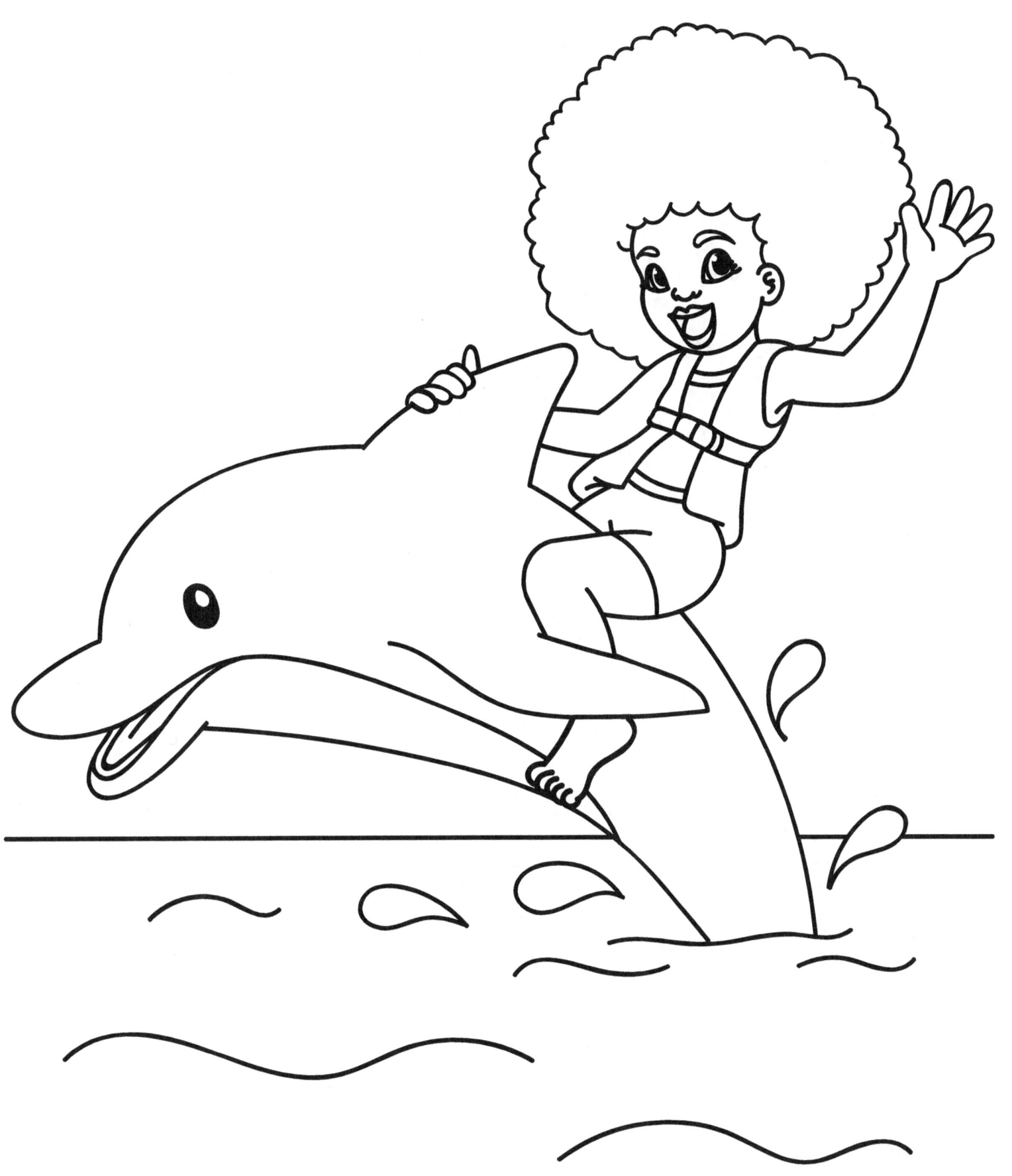

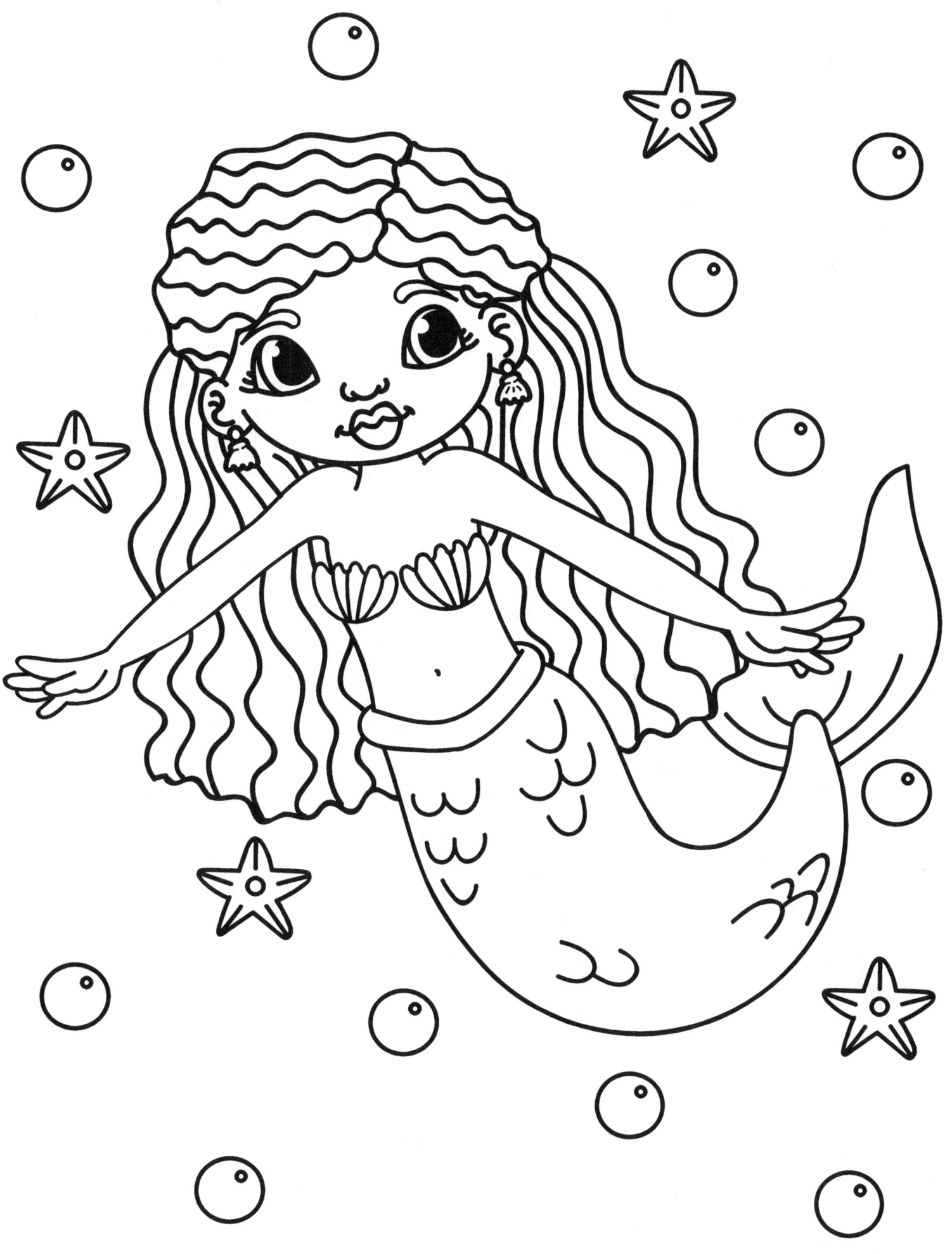

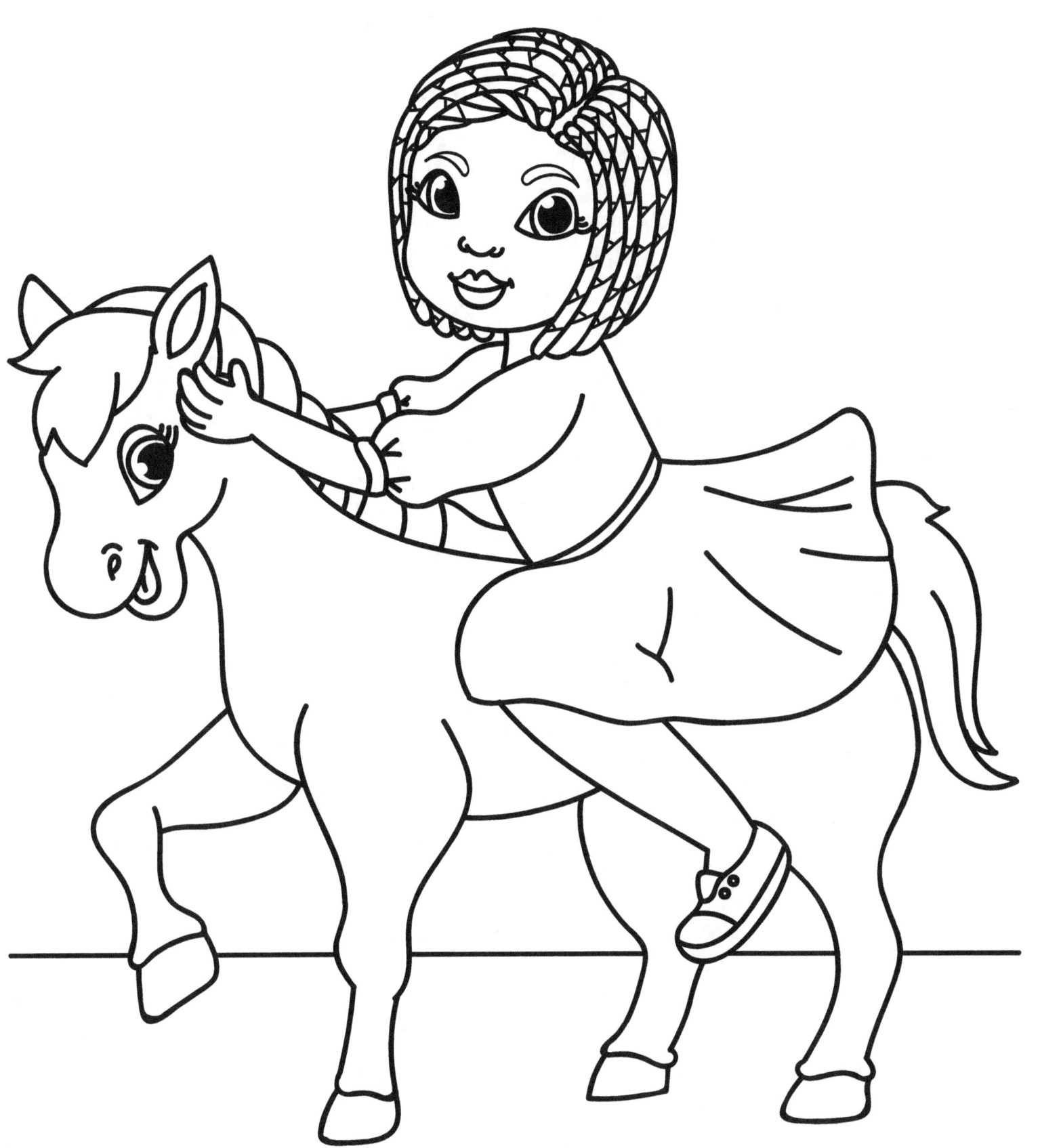

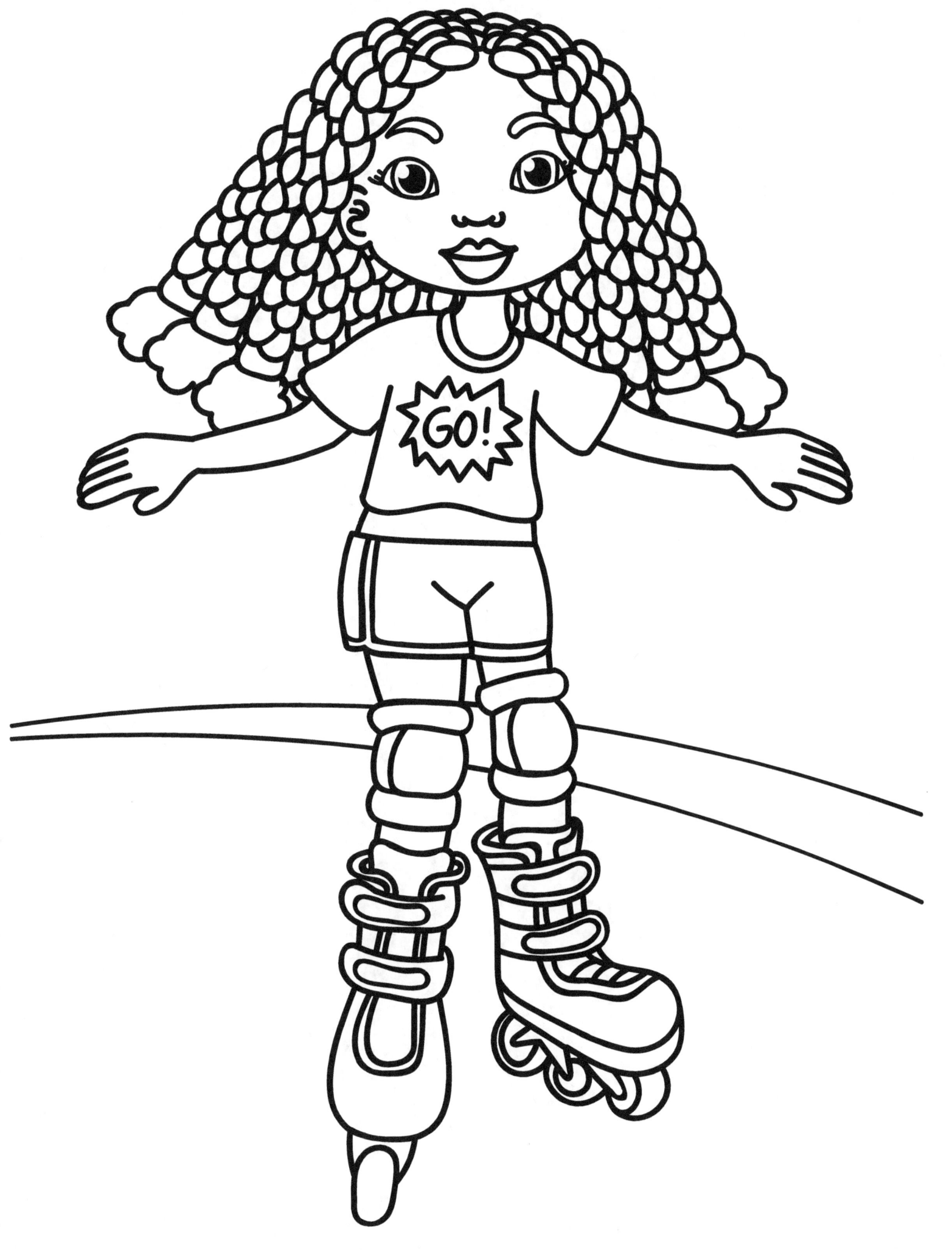

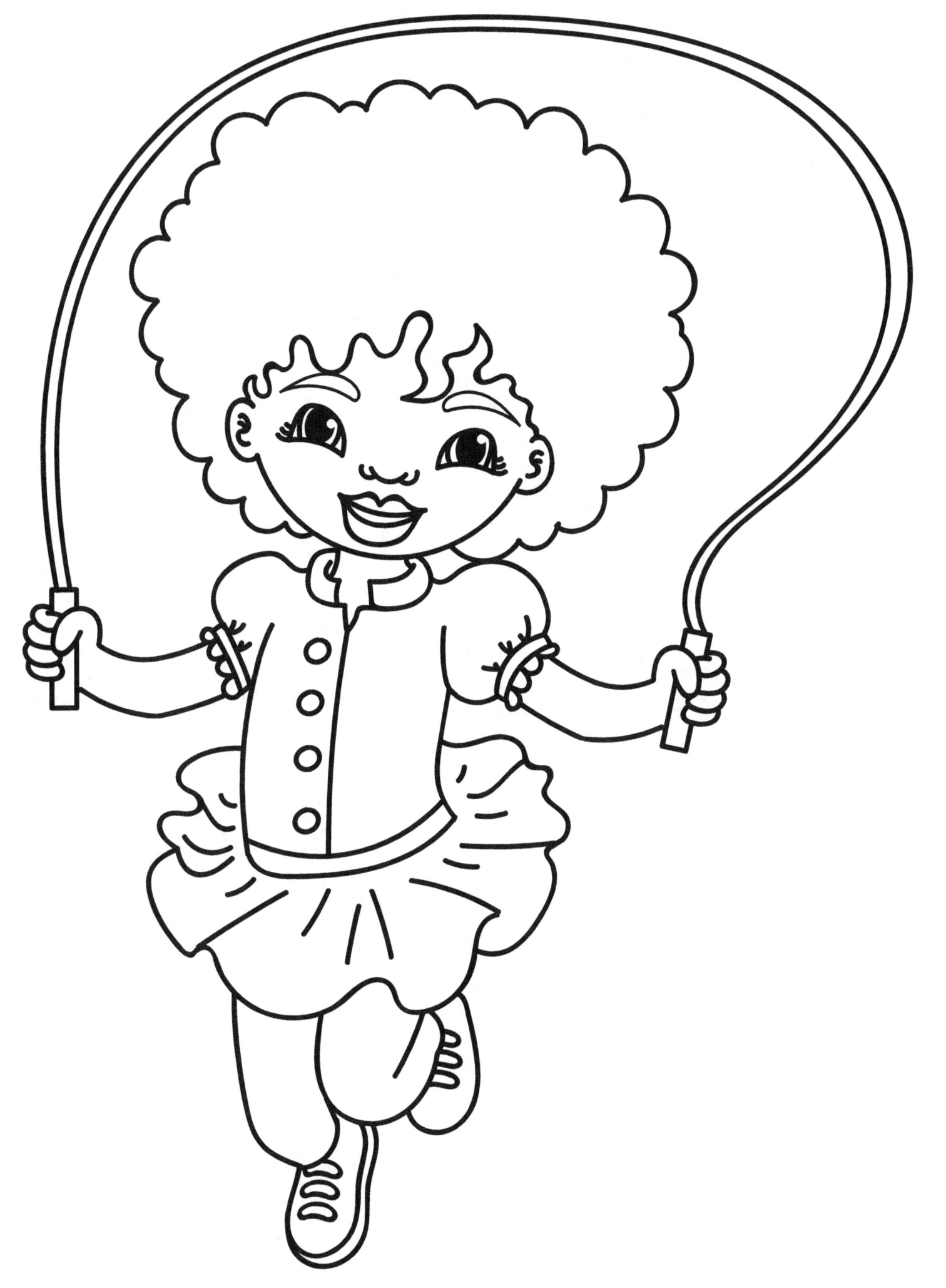

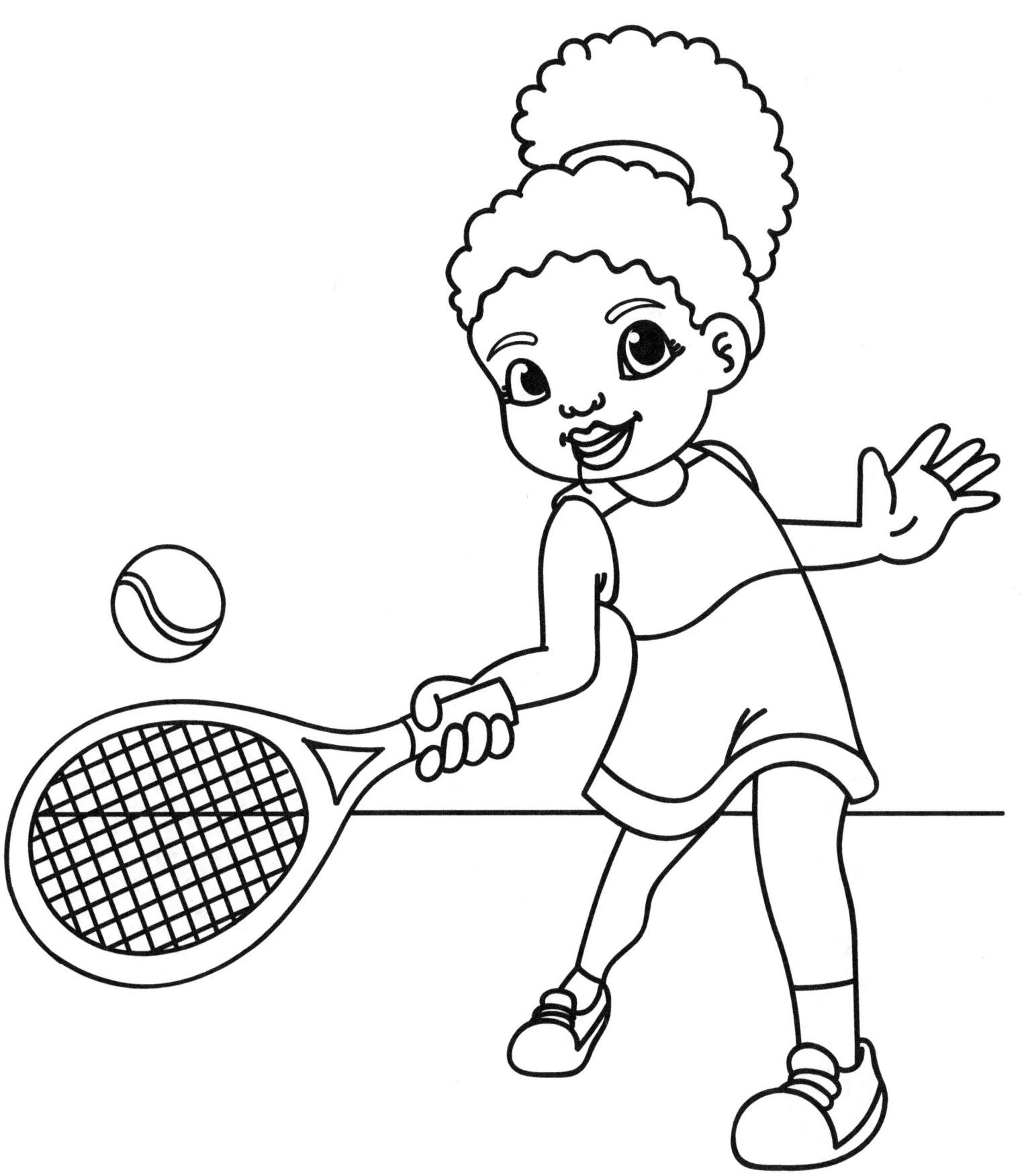

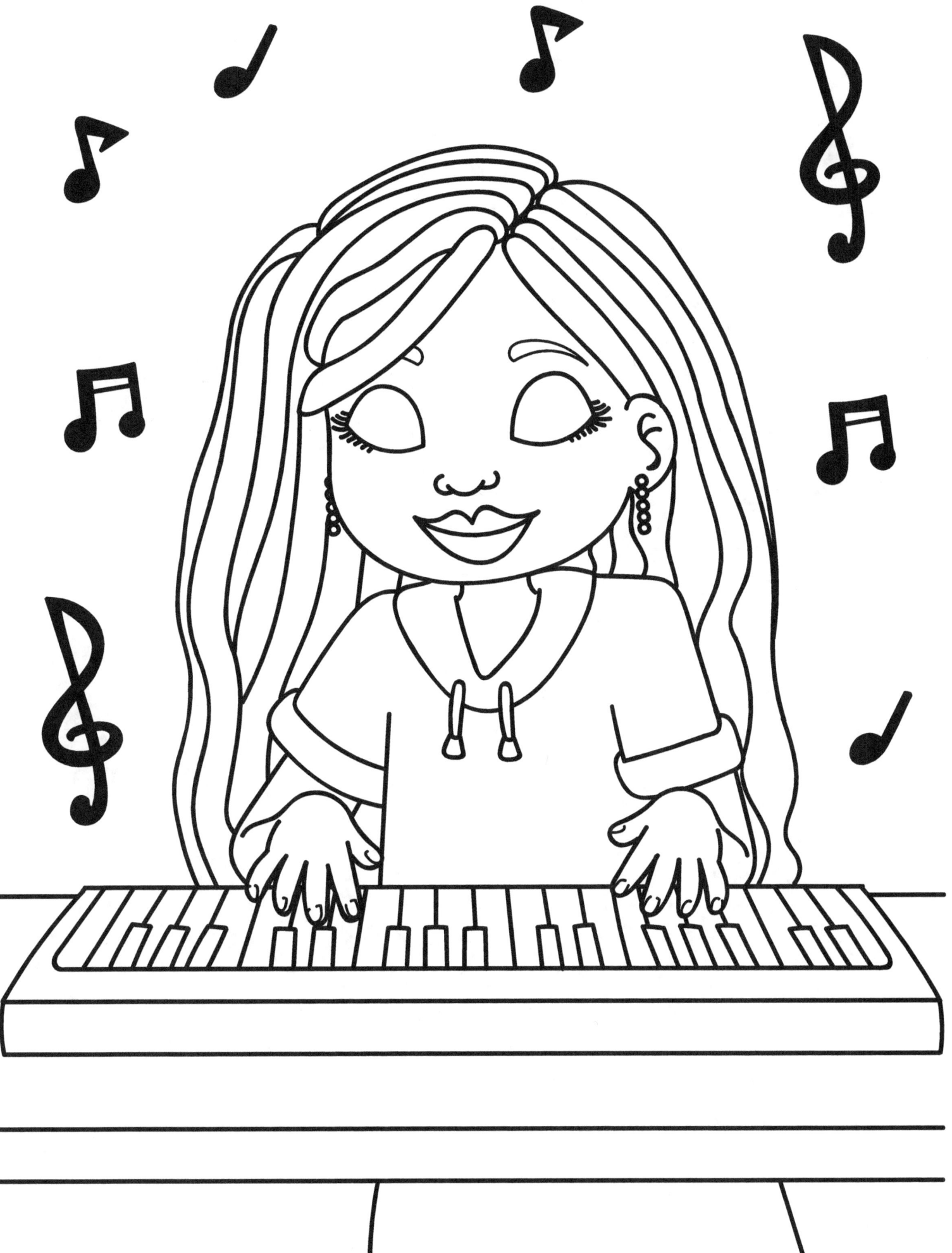

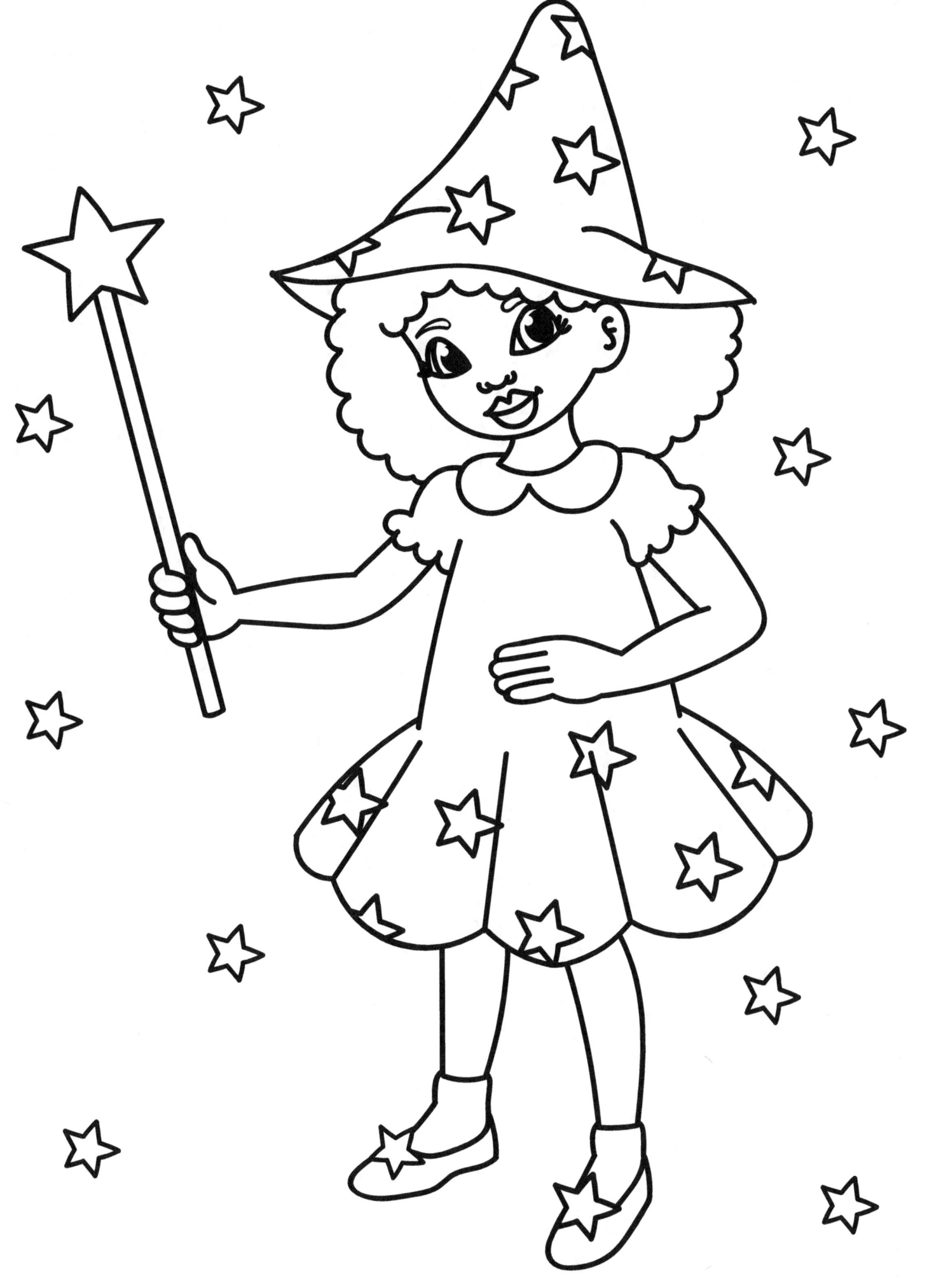

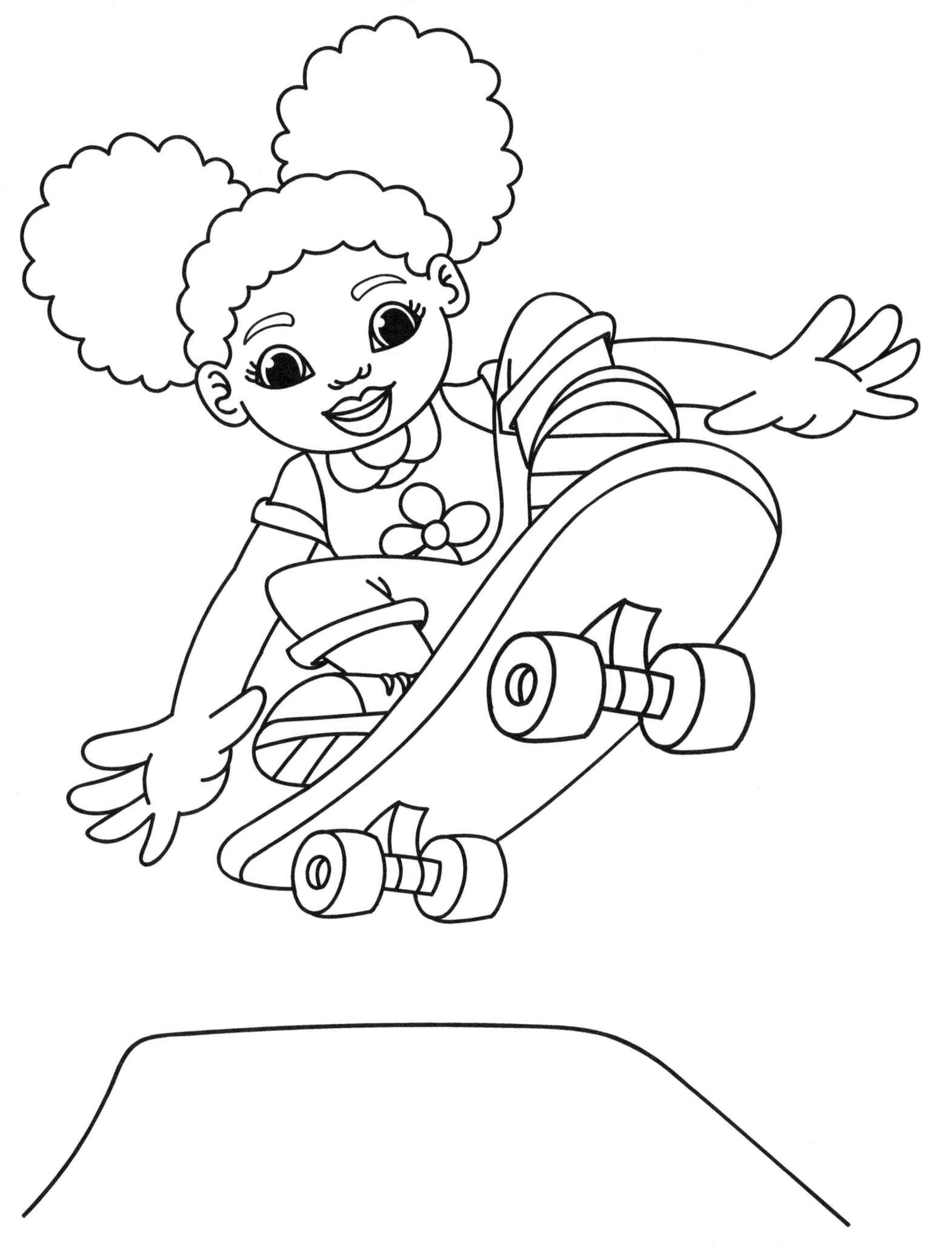

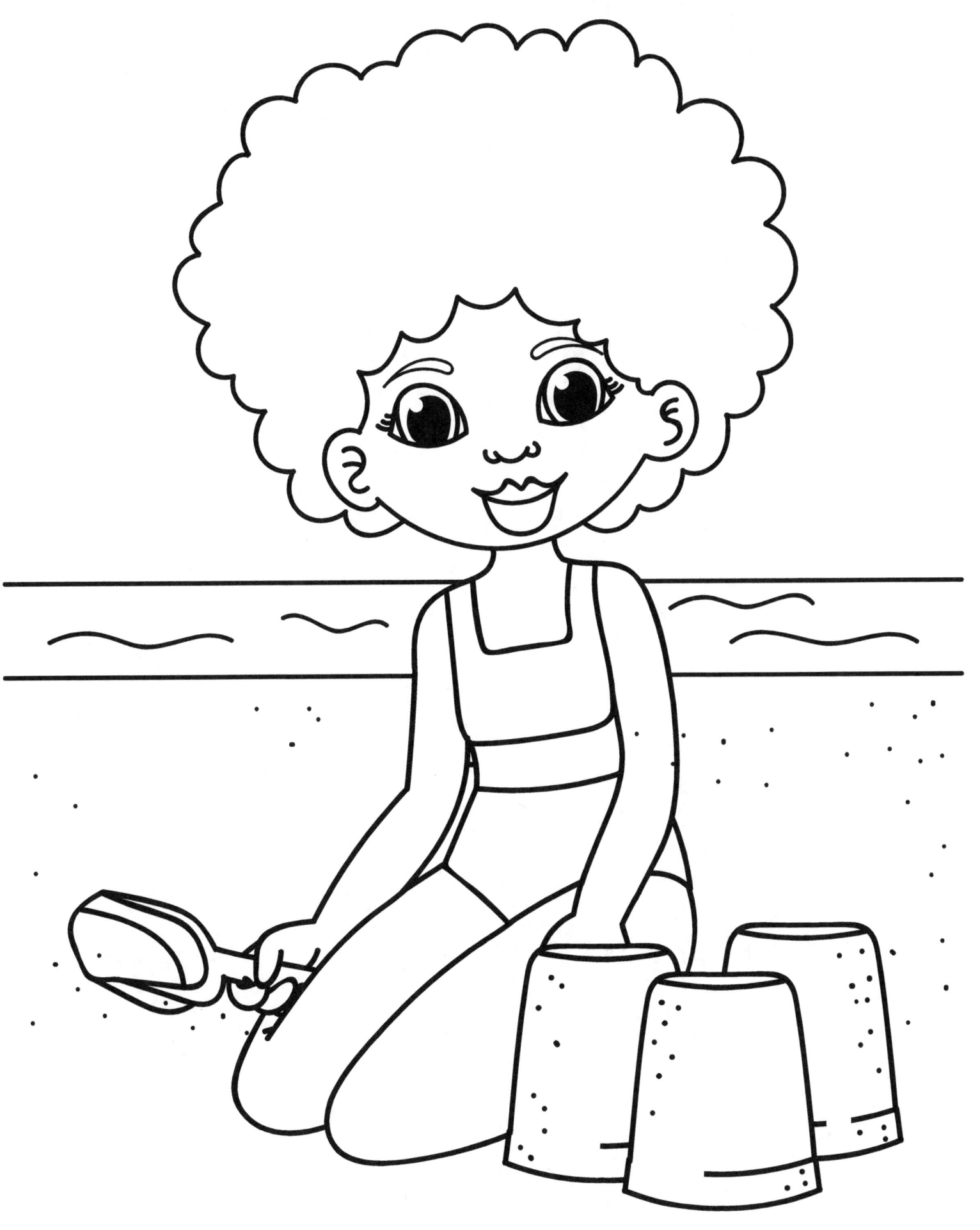

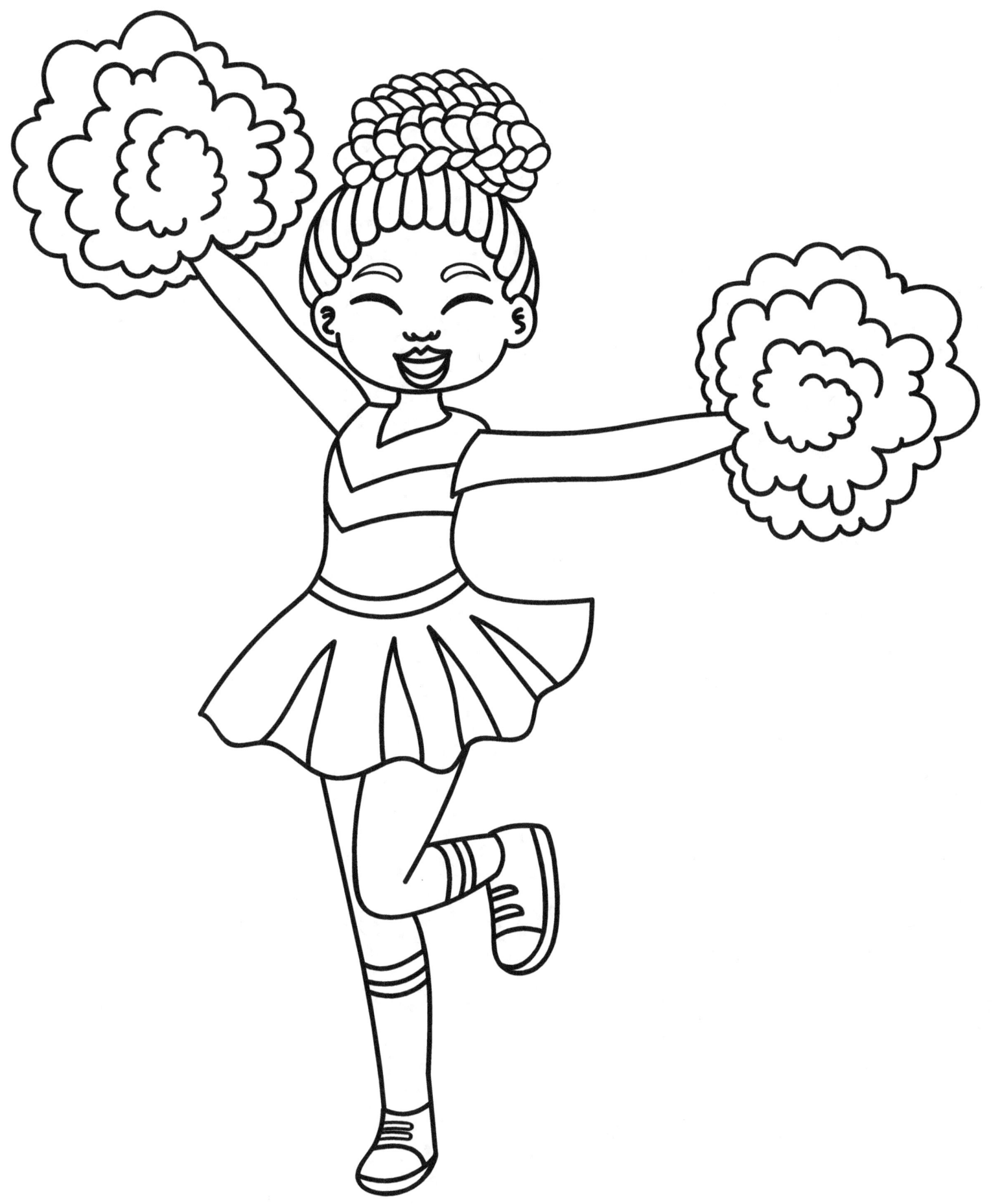

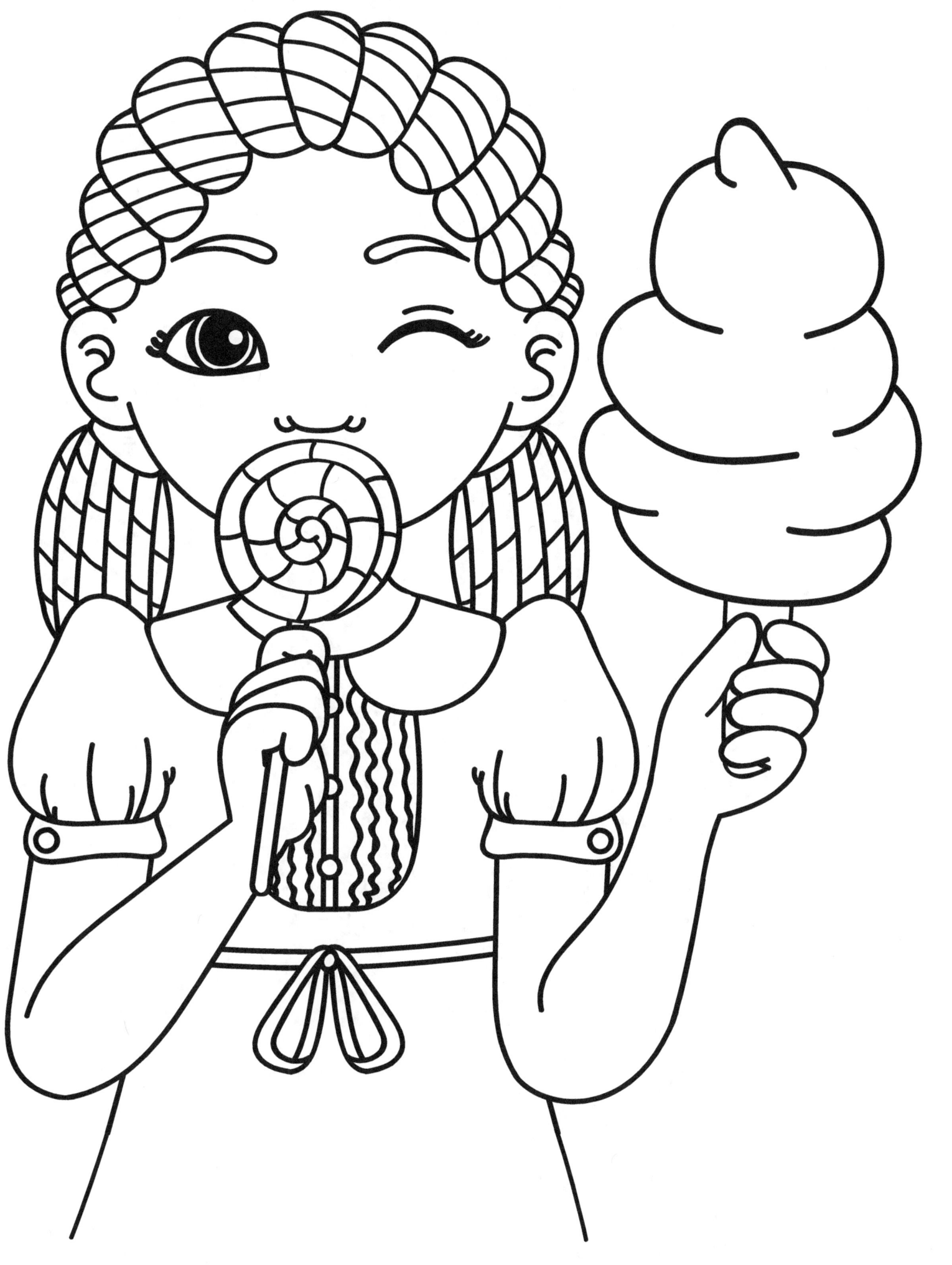

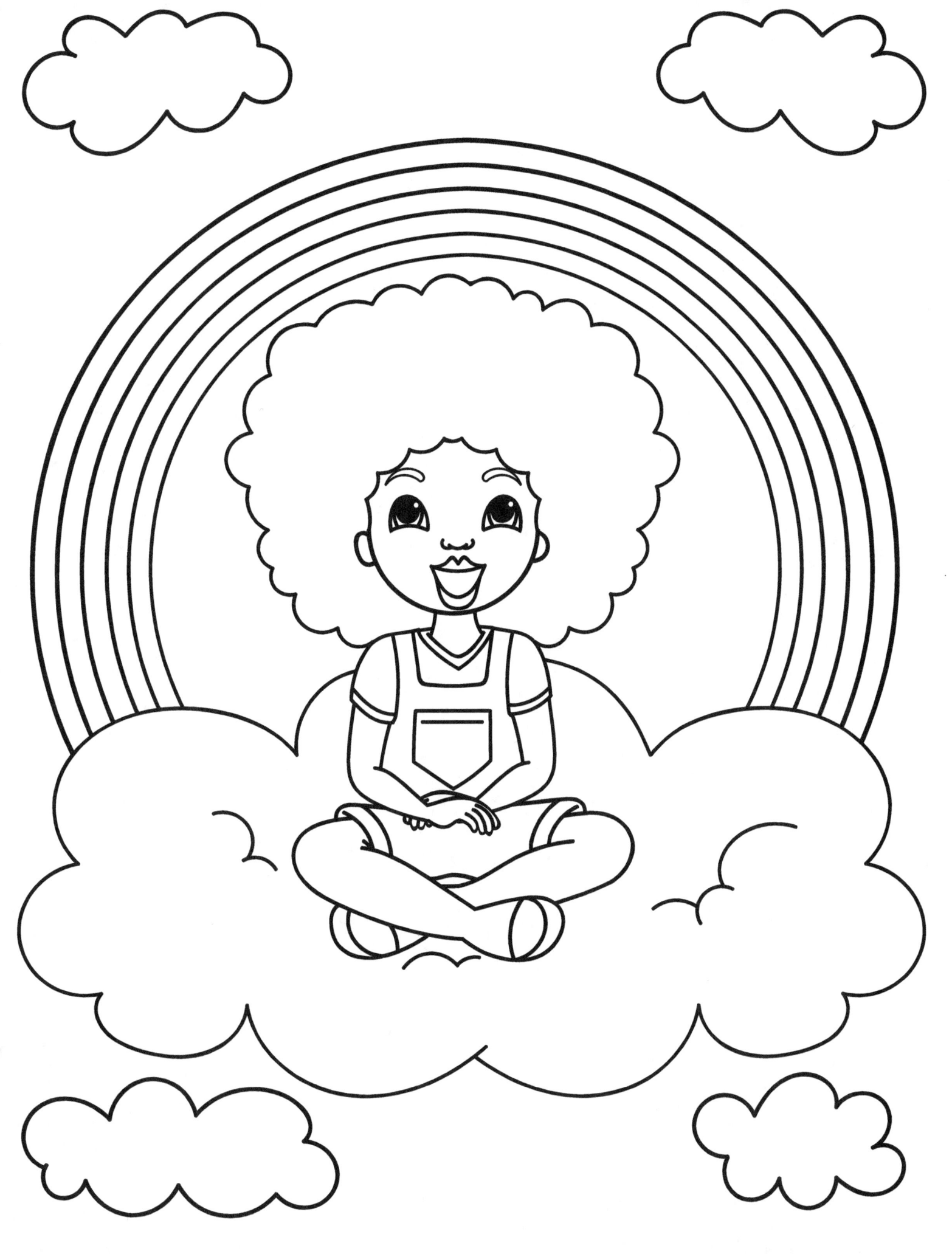

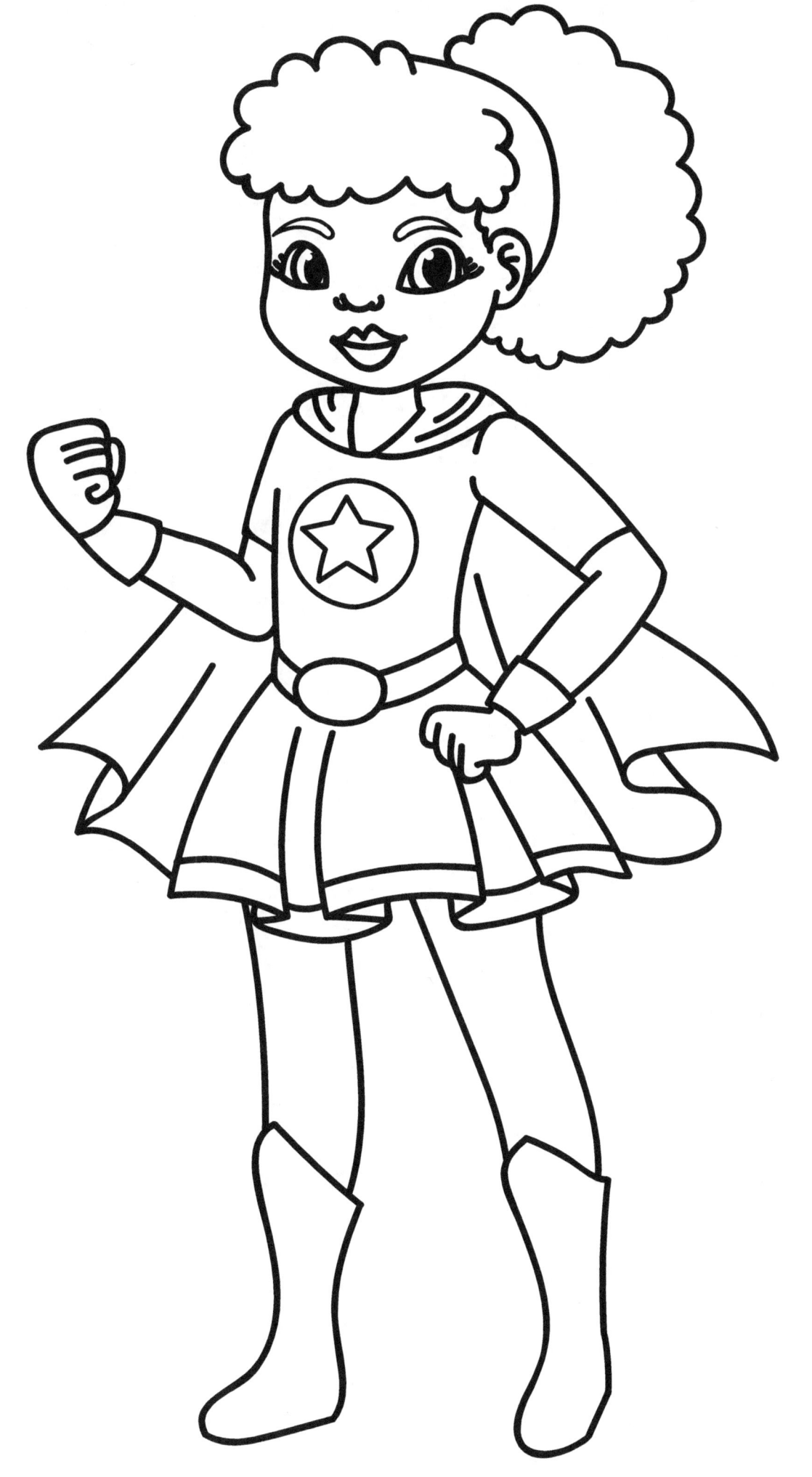

...HOPE YOU HAD A GREAT TIME WITH US...

We would be happy to color with you again soon.

It would be amazing if you wrote an honest product review on Amazon. It only takes 1-2 minutes and means a lot to us!

QUESTIONS, REQUESTS, OR FEEDBACK?

Write us an email: baldehmarketing@gmail.com